Editor
Mary S. Jones, M.A.

Cover Artist
Delia Rubio

Editor in Chief
Karen J. Goldfluss, M.S. Ed.

Illustrator
Jan D'Silva

Art Production Manager
Kevin Barnes

Imaging
Leonard P. Swierski

Publisher
Mary D. Smith, M.S. Ed.

WRITE fr...

Writing Lessons

Writing Models & Activities

PRACTICE WRITING...
- Narratives
- Information Reports
- Humorous Verse
- Recounts
- Descriptions
- Speeches
- Explanations
- Procedures
- Research Projects

... and more!

Teacher Created Resources

Author

Jane Baker

Teacher Created Resources, Inc.
6421 Industry Way
Westminster, CA 92683
www.teachercreated.com

ISBN: 978-1-4206-8072-0

© 2008 Teacher Created Resources, Inc.
Made in U.S.A.

Teacher Created Resources

TABLE OF CONTENTS

Write from the Start! Writing Lessons helps students with the kind of writing they do every day. Each lesson looks at a different type of writing. Some are imaginative text types, such as narratives and poems. Others are factual text types, such as reports and explanations.

All lessons begin with a sample text, which serves as a lesson model or for students to use as a reference when applying a strategy to their own writing. It is important that the text and special features of the sample models are read and discussed with students. (Note: Many of the sample texts used throughout the book have been written by students, which will make them even more enjoyable for your students to read and analyze.)

After the sample model has been introduced, students can work through the activities that follow. These give them guidance and practice in writing a similar type of text. The first activities in each lesson ask students to focus on the context of the sample model and reflect on what they read and how it was written. Additional activities direct students to the grammar and punctuation used in the model and how these apply to the text. Lessons also include activities that help students with vocabulary meaning and spelling. Every lesson ends with a "Your Turn to Write" section, where students apply what they have learned. This can serve as a reflection or assessment tool for each lesson.

In addition to the space provided on the activity pages of this book, it is recommended that students have their own journals or writer's notebooks. These can be used for some of the writing activities at the end of most lessons, where students may wish to extend their writing. A journal or notebook is also a good place for students to add references (illustrations, advertisements, photographs, research information, etc.) that they collect for future writing.

If you plan to use all of the lessons in the book, it is best to work through the book from Lesson 1 to the end. This will allow students to build on skills from one lesson to the next. However, each lesson can be taught independently. You may even wish to focus on a group of lessons that meet specific needs or standards. In either case, the format of this book allows for flexibility.

The activities in this book meet the following writing standards, which are used with permission from McREL. Reading standards are also met by the "What Did You Read?" and "How Is It Written?" sections of each lesson; however, those standards are not listed below.

Copyright 2006 McREL. Mid-continent Research for Education and Learning.
Address: 2250 S. Parker Road, Suite 500, Aurora, CO 80014
Telephone: 303-377-0990 Website: *www.mcrel.org/standards-benchmarks*

Standard 1. Uses the general skills and strategies of the writing process

1. Prewriting: Uses prewriting strategies to plan written work (Pages 11, 18, 19, 25, 31, 37, 43, 49, 55, 62, 63, 70, 73)
2. Drafting and Revising: Uses strategies to draft and revise written work (Pages 11,18, 19, 25, 31, 37, 41, 43, 49, 55, 62, 63, 70, 73)
3. Editing and Publishing: Uses strategies to edit and publish written work (Pages 11, 18, 19, 25, 31, 37, 43, 49, 55, 62, 63, 70, 73)
4. Evaluates own and others' writing (Pages 13, 21, 27, 33, 39, 43, 51, 57, 65, 72)
6. Uses strategies to write for a variety of purposes (Pages 25, 26, 32, 43, 44, 50, 62, 63, 64, 71)
7. Writes expository compositions (Pages 6, 38, 56)
8. Writes narrative accounts, such as poems and stories (Pages 12, 18, 20)
10. Writes expressive compositions (Pages 55, 70))

Standard 2. Uses the stylistic and rhetorical aspects of writing

1. Uses descriptive language that clarifies and enhances ideas (Page 24)
2. Uses paragraph form in writing (Pages 31, 37, 41, 63)
3. Uses a variety of sentence structures in writing (Pages 9, 35)

Standard 3. Uses grammatical and mechanical conventions in written compositions

3. Uses nouns in written compositions (Pages 15, 67)
4. Uses verbs in written compositions (Pages 7, 29, 53, 67)
5. Uses adjectives in written compositions (Pages 10, 23, 54)
6. Uses adverbs in written compositions (Pages 7, 41, 42, 47, 59)
9. Uses conventions of spelling in written compositions (Pages 8, 14, 22, 28, 34, 40, 46, 52, 58, 61, 66)
10. Uses conventions of capitalization in written compositions (Pages 9, 60, 68)
11. Uses conventions of punctuation in written compositions (Pages 16, 23, 29, 35, 47, 53, 60, 68)

Standard 4. Gathers and uses information for research purposes

1. Uses a variety of strategies to plan research (Page 73)
2. Uses encyclopedias to gather information for research topics (Pages 31, 49)
3. Uses dictionaries to gather information for research topics (Page 30)

Dear Student,

When you use this book, you will practice recognizing and writing many of the text types you learn at school. Several of the sample texts have been written by students in fourth grade and are good examples of what a fourth-grade student can achieve.

Carefully read the sample text at the beginning of each lesson. Check what special features of the writing are highlighted or have arrows pointing to them as you read. Then work through the questions and the exercises that follow.

Work through the lessons in order, from 1 to 11. This will allow you to build on the skills learned from lesson to lesson. By the end of the year, you will have a good understanding of fourth-grade language and writing skills.

You will need a good dictionary, a folder to keep your writing organized and clean, and a quiet place with good light in which to work.

Good luck, and have fun.

Jane Baker
Author

When we write a **recount**, we are telling **what happened in chronological sequence**.

STRUCTURE

LANGUAGE

Setting tells time and place

Comparison helps reader to "see" the peaks

Time words to make sequence clear

Personal comments on facts

Sequenced events in paragraphs

Good choice of adjective

Examples of viciousness

Conclusion looks forward to next stage of journey

Time word

Interesting comparison

OUR TRIP TO NEW ZEALAND

On Thursday we crossed the Southern Alps. It took hours. We drove through Arthur's Pass and then stopped to look at the mountains. The peaks looked a bit like black-and-white pictures, with their bright, white snow and big, black rocks. We stayed overnight in Greymouth, where we bought some books.

Yesterday, we drove on to see the famous Franz Josef Glacier. First we left our things in our motel, and then we set out to walk to the glacier. It took a long, long time to walk over the stones in the bottom of the valley, and when we got to the wall of the glacier, we were very thirsty. We broke off a tiny bit of glacial ice and sucked it. We were drinking water that was thousands of years old. It was much nicer than sucking ice from the fridge.

Today, we drove to the Fox Glacier. Someone had told Dad about a lake on the way, so we went there first. We had to walk through a dark forest to find Lake Matheson. It was a very cold lake because all of its water came from the glacier.

By the time we got to the Fox Glacier valley, it was too late in the day to reach the glacier itself. We stayed in the parking lot to watch great big, green-brown parrots called *keas*. They were vicious. They were walking all over the cars in the parking lot, ripping up soft parts with their beaks. They chewed up windshield wipers. We even saw one pecking the air valves on tires to deflate them.

Tomorrow, we have to get up early because we are flying to the top of Franz Josef in a ski-plane. I am looking forward to that because the top of the glacier is all deep snow. So far we have only seen the front ends of glaciers, and they are like huge walls of blue-green ice with brown streaks in them.

Penny (age 9)

✹ WHAT DID YOU READ?

① **Circle** the correct answer. Crossing the Southern Alps did not take very long. **True / False**

② **Circle** the correct answer. The travelers stayed overnight in . . .

   a. Arthur's Pass   **b.** Greymouth   **c.** Lake Matheson

③ **Circle** the correct answer. The thirsty travelers drank icy water from . . .

   a. Lake Matheson   **b.** Fox Glacier   **c.** Franz Josef Glacier

④ **Circle** the correct answer. The water in Lake Matheson comes from . . .

   a. a glacier   **b.** a river   **c.** the sea

⑤ **Circle** the most complete answer. Keas . . .

   a. look like green-brown parrots

   b. are large, green parrots with big beaks

   c. look like big, green-brown parrots

   d. are big, green-brown parrots that have vicious habits

⑥ **Explain** in your own words what you would see at the end of a glacier.

_____

_____

⑦ If the ice is blue-green because it is so deep and thick, can you **explain** why it has brown streaks in it? (*Clue:* Think about what the glacier is moving through.)

_____

_____

✹ HOW IS IT WRITTEN?

① Time words (adverbs of time) make the sequence (order of happening) clear.
Write at least two time words used in the text.

_____   _____

② Recounts are usually written in the past tense. **Find** three verbs written in the
past tense in the first paragraph.

_____   _____   _____   _____

③ In the first paragraph, the writer uses a comparison to help us see the mountain peaks.
Complete this comparison: They looked a bit like _____.

④ Recount writing contains facts. **Write** one fact about keas that you find in paragraph 4.

_____

⊚ SPELLING AND MEANING

Word Box	sequence	bought	peak	tire
	diary	brought	peek	tiring
	dairy	glacier	glacial	

When you learn spelling, **look** at the word, **cover** the word, **write** the word, and **check** your spelling. Practice this method as often as it takes to get it right.

① Some words are spelled a lot like other words but have completely different meanings. **Circle** the correct word in these sentences.

   a. Eddie **bought / brought** a book on glaciers from the new bookshop.

   b. It is not polite to **peak / peek** at birthday presents early.

   c. Lucy writes in her **diary / dairy** every morning.

   d. Snow chains help prevent car **tiring / tires** from skidding when driving through snow.

   e. Mt. Kosciusko is 7,310 feet high at its **peek / peak**.

   f. New Zealand is famous for its **diary / dairy** cows and their cream.

② **Sequence** means "in order." Read these lists. If they are in correct sequence, write **Y** in the space provided. If they are out of sequence, write **N**.

   a. Dressing: coat, shirt, trousers, socks _____

   b. Apple-eating: remove seeds, peel, eat, cut _____

   c. Mowing: start mower, cut grass, put gas in tank _____

   d. Catch bus: board bus, pay fare, find seat, sit down _____

③ The sound **er** (*glacier*) can be spelled in many ways (e.g., **ear**ly, **cur**ly, **sir**, **wor**ld). Can you **complete** this table using these same spelling patterns?

H __ __ D	WH __ __ L	F __ __	H __ __ __ D
(cows)	(spin)	(cat coat)	(the ear did it)
F __ __ N	B __ __ D	F __ __ L	P __ __ __ L
(a plant)	(sparrow)	(to roll a flag)	(jewel)

④ **Label** the following pictures with a word from the table above.

a. _____   **b.** _____   **c.** _____

✺ GRAMMAR

A **simple sentence** contains a subject, a verb, and an object.

Example: **Penny** (subject) **explored** (verb) **the glacier** (object).

A **compound sentence** contains two or more equally important **Subject → Verb → Object** patterns joined by a **comma** and the word **and**, **or**, or **but**.

Examples: Penny explored the glacier, **but** her mother studied plants **and** her father took photographs.

The travelers could climb to the top of the glacier, **or** they could fly there.

① **Underline** the subject, **circle** the verb, and **double-underline** the object in each of these sentences.

   a. Glaciers are rivers of ice.   **b.** Harry climbed the glacier wall.

   c. A glacier climber carries rope, spikes, and a small hammer.

② **Rearrange** the words in each exercise to form a **complete simple sentence**.

   a. very cold mountain lakes The waters of are

   _____

   b. Snowboarding popular sports in the Alps and skiing are

   _____

   c. very thin Mountain air is _____

③ **Join** these simple sentences to make compound sentences using a comma and the word **but**.

   a. Glaciers carry stones in their ice. Rivers carry silt in their waters.

   _____

   b. Glaciers begin in alpine lakes. Rivers begin in mountain rains.

   _____

   c. Thin ice looks white. Thick ice looks blue or green.

   _____

✺ PUNCTUATION

Sentences start with **capital letters**, and so do titles (e.g., **Doctor**, **General**) and proper nouns (specific names of people and places, such as **Julia** and **Egypt**).

Example: **S**ir **E**dmund **H**ilary and **T**enzing **N**orgay were the first people to reach the peak of **M**t. **E**verest.

Circle all the letters that should be capitalized in this passage.

some mountains are famous for their snow—mountains like everest in nepal, fuji in japan, the matterhorn in austria, and tongariro in new zealand. other mountains, like mt. st. helens in the united states, vesuvius in italy, pinatubo in the philippines, and gunung agung in indonesia, are volcanic and famous for boiling lava and explosions.

FUN WITH WORDS

① This is a "chill-factor scale." Can you **arrange** the words in the box on this scale from warmer at the bottom to colder at the top?

colder

_____

_____

_____

_____

_____

warmer

| cold |
| chilly |
| mild |
| icy |
| cool |

② **Choose** a word from the "chill-factor scale" that best describes these scenes.

a. _____   **b.** _____   **c.** _____

③ These are all water words. Can you **complete** them? Use a dictionary, if needed.

a. a river of ice: G __ __ C __ __ __

b. a small body of water surrounded by land: L __ K __

c. a boomerang-shaped lake near a river: B __ L L __ B __ NG

d. the ebb and flow of water on the beach: T __ __ E

④ Getting around in alpine country (high, snowy mountain country) requires special vehicles and equipment. Can you **unscramble** the names of these alpine vehicles and tools?

KISS	long, narrow footwear for snow travel	S_____
DELS	dog-drawn cart on steel runners	S_____
GGANTOBO	a small downhill speedster	T_____
AIRCH FILT	a seated lift up the mountain	C_____ _____

⑤ Who am I? I am an animal with four legs. I have a hairy coat and a beard. I have handsome curling horns, and I am famous for my ability to climb steep mountain sides. I eat tiny alpine plants and summer grasses. My wife, strangely, is called Nanny, even when we are young.

I am a __ __ __ __ __ __ __ __ __ __ __ __ __.

LESSON 1: WRITING A RECOUNT

•••••••••••••••••••••*Teacher Created Resources, Inc.*•••*Write from the Start! Writing Lessons*••••••••••

☼ YOUR TURN TO WRITE

> **TIP FOR TOP WRITERS!**
> When writing a recount, list all the events in the correct sequence. Then **write** your recount in that order.

① **List** these morning events in their **correct sequence**.

eat	1.
wake	2.
dress	3.
wash	4.
brush teeth	5.

② Look at Jenny's sequence of events. Can you help her **put** them in the **correct order** so she can recount how she got stuck up a tree?

I climbed higher	1.
cat climbed higher	2.
cat raced up tree	3.
dog chased my cat	4.
cat wouldn't come down	5.
I climbed tree	6.
both too frightened to climb down	7.

③ Choose **two** of the following topics and write a **sequence of events** for each.

    a. When I fell in the river   **b.** When the truck tipped over   **c.** When I spilled the milk

_____

_____

_____

④ Now **choose** an interesting event that has happened in your life and then, on a separate sheet of paper, **write** a recount of what happened. Proofread it for spelling and punctuation errors. Make sure you have not used the same word too often. Then write a neat, clean copy to turn in.

When we write a **narrative**, we are telling a story. It can be an imaginative story like this one, or it can be a story set in the real world.

STRUCTURE

LANGUAGE

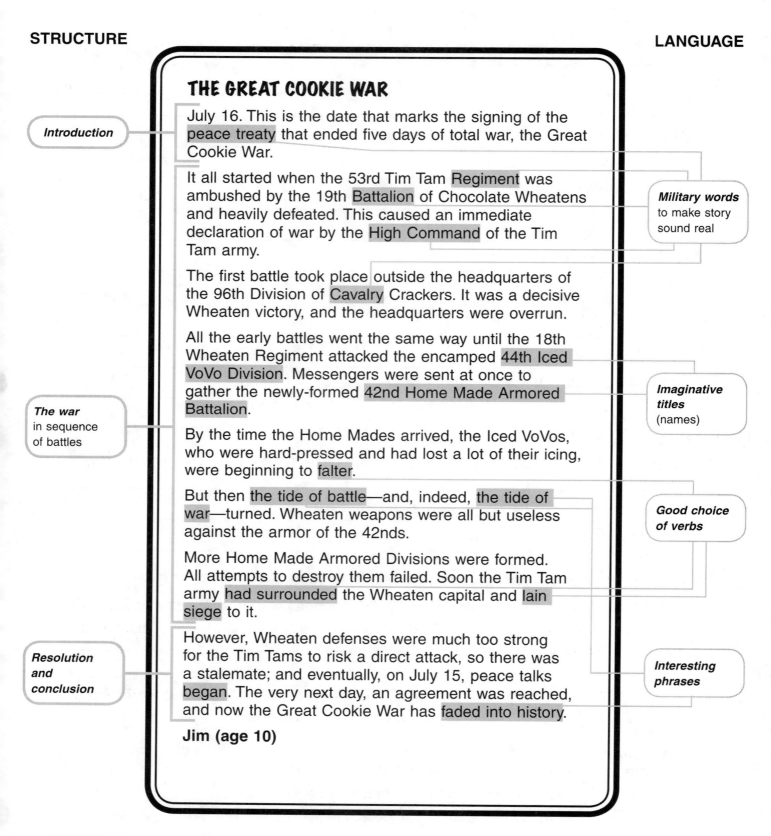

THE GREAT COOKIE WAR

Introduction

July 16. This is the date that marks the signing of the peace treaty that ended five days of total war, the Great Cookie War.

It all started when the 53rd Tim Tam Regiment was ambushed by the 19th Battalion of Chocolate Wheatens and heavily defeated. This caused an immediate declaration of war by the High Command of the Tim Tam army.

Military words to make story sound real

The first battle took place outside the headquarters of the 96th Division of Cavalry Crackers. It was a decisive Wheaten victory, and the headquarters were overrun.

All the early battles went the same way until the 18th Wheaten Regiment attacked the encamped 44th Iced VoVo Division. Messengers were sent at once to gather the newly-formed 42nd Home Made Armored Battalion.

Imaginative titles (names)

The war in sequence of battles

By the time the Home Mades arrived, the Iced VoVos, who were hard-pressed and had lost a lot of their icing, were beginning to falter.

But then the tide of battle—and, indeed, the tide of war—turned. Wheaten weapons were all but useless against the armor of the 42nds.

Good choice of verbs

More Home Made Armored Divisions were formed. All attempts to destroy them failed. Soon the Tim Tam army had surrounded the Wheaten capital and lain siege to it.

Resolution and conclusion

However, Wheaten defenses were much too strong for the Tim Tams to risk a direct attack, so there was a stalemate; and eventually, on July 15, peace talks began. The very next day, an agreement was reached, and now the Great Cookie War has faded into history.

Interesting phrases

Jim (age 10)

WHAT DID YOU READ?

① **Circle** the correct answer.

July 16 was the day the Great Cookie War started. **True / False**

② Who started the war? _____

③ **Name** the two sides in the war.

a. the _____ army   **b.** the _____ army

④ **Circle** the correct word.

All the early battles were **victories / defeats** for the Tim Tams.

⑤ **Circle** the correct answer. The tide of battle changed . . .

a. after the Cavalry Crackers' headquarters battle

b. when the 88th Wheaten Regiment attacked the encamped Iced VoVos

c. when the Armored Home Mades entered the war

⑥ **Circle** the correct answer.

"The Tim Tam Army *lain siege* to the Wheaten capital." This means . . .

a. The walls of the capital were surrounded and could not be exited.

b. The capital was entered by the Tim Tams.

c. The capital was burned.

⑦ **Circle** the correct answer. The war lasted . . .

a. fifteen days   **b.** five days   **c.** six days

HOW IS IT WRITTEN?

① **Circle** the correct answer. The story starts with a date and tells us how long the war lasted. This orientation . . .

a. gives us a time frame for the story

b. needs more information

c. is not important in the story

② **Complete** this sentence.

The writer has described the battles of the war in chronological S ___ QU ___ ___ CE.

③ The writer gives a military feel to his story by using technical words that soldiers use. **Write** three examples of these words from the text.

_____   _____   _____

④ This is a humorous story. What makes it funny? **Circle** the **two** most correct answers.

a. use of imaginative cookie brand names for army units

b. funny things that happen in the story

c. description of the losses suffered by the Iced VoVos (their icing)

⑤ **Circle** the correct answer. The writer links the end of his story to the beginning of his story . . .

a. with the peace treaty   **b.** with the Wheaten defenses   **c.** with the stalemate

✺ SPELLING AND MEANING

Word Box	sign	armor	headquarters	weapon
	siege	capital	falter	declaration
	icing	cookie	useless	decisive

To make some long words easier to spell, we can break them into two words (e.g., head/quarters). We can break other long words into **syllables** for easier spelling (e.g., cap/i/tal).

① **Break** each of these words into **syllables**.

a. cookie _____

b. icing _____

c. falter _____

d. declaration _____

e. decisive _____

f. useless _____

② Dictionaries are valuable tools for writers. To use them you must know how to arrange words alphabetically.

a. **Arrange** these words according to where their **first** letter comes in the alphabet:

capital	armor	icing

_____

b. If the first letters are the same, arrange the words according to their **second** letters. **Arrange** these words alphabetically:

division	defeat	dangerous

_____

c. Using the rules above, **number** these pictures 1–4 as they occur in the alphabet.

  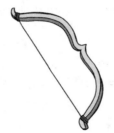 

_____ _____ _____ _____

d. If the first and second letters are the same, look at the **third** letters. **Arrange** these words alphabetically:

sign	siege	single

_____

⊚ SPELLING AND MEANING (cont.)

e. Arrange these words as you would find them in a dictionary:

falter	weapon	decisive	declaration	useless

_____

③ **–or** is a common spelling pattern (e.g., arm**or**). Can you **complete** these **–or** words?

a. Making jokes and being funny: H ___ MOR

b. Very loud noises all together: CL ___ MOR

c. Strength and good health: V ___ GOR

⊚ GRAMMAR

Nouns name things. There are many kinds of nouns. You already know about common nouns (e.g., gate, friend, house) and proper nouns (e.g., John, Korea, July).

Here are two more types of nouns.

Group or **collective nouns** are words that name a whole **group** of creatures or things.

Examples: a <u>regiment</u> of soldiers, a <u>flock</u> of sheep

Abstract nouns name **ideas** and **feelings** (things that we know exist but cannot see).

Examples: bravery, happiness, victory

① Name the kind of underlined nouns in these sentences.

a. Police and firefighters are well known for their <u>courage</u>. _____

b. The <u>battalion</u> marched across the parade ground. _____

c. A <u>swarm</u> of bees has settled in that big tree. _____

d. The <u>choir</u> sang with such <u>sweetness</u> that the <u>audience</u> wept.

_____   _____   _____

② **Insert** a group noun from the box into each sentence below. You will not need all of the words. If needed, use an encyclopedia to help you.

congregation	school	pack	mob	flock	fleet	herd	clutch

a. A _____ of chickens were all gathered around their mother hen.

b. The _____ of wolves loped silently across the snow.

c. A cyclone scattered the _____ of yachts.

d. A _____ of tiny fish swirled in the waters off the reef.

e. The church _____ all enjoyed the Christmas service.

GRAMMAR (cont.)

③ **Circle** the abstract noun in each sentence.

   a. Mr. Venturini was known for his generosity to people in need.

   b. An army commander must show leadership in the field.

   c. The warrior showed mercy to his enemy.

   d. A true gentleman is known for his courtesy to everyone.

PUNCTUATION

Sentences end with a **period** (.) if they **tell** us something, they end with a **question mark** (?) if they **ask** something, and they end with an **exclamation mark** (!) if they express a **sudden emotion** like surprise or alarm.

   Examples: Canada and Mexico border the United States**.**

   How many islands are there in Indonesia**?**

   Ouch! Ouch! It hurts!

Insert all of the missing punctuation.

   a. Is India north or south of the equator

   b. Good heavens That pink pig is flying

   c. Chile's flag is sky blue with a big yellow sun in the middle

   d. What is the national language of Brazil

FUN WITH WORDS

① Can you **match** these groups with the group noun that names them?

a.	lions	herd
b.	whales	team
c.	grapes	pod
d.	cattle	army
e.	caterpillars	bunch
f.	football players	pride

② You can have great fun inventing new group nouns (e.g., a **giggle** of girls, a **boast** of boys, an **argument** of lawyers). See if you can **invent** group nouns to name these groups. Think about what the groups do most together.

   a. a _____ of teachers   **b.** a _____ of ducks

   c. a _____ of racing cars   **d.** a _____ of gossips

   e. a _____ of snakes

☼ FUN WITH WORDS (cont.)

③ In the military, some people have more authority than others. They have titles to show their places in the line of authority. The same happens in most organizations. Can you **arrange** these people in order of authority in their organizations, with the **higher-ranked person first**?

    a. sailors: seaman, admiral, captain

    _____

    b. school people: vice principal, student, teacher, principal

    _____

    c. government people: senator, mayor, governor, president

    _____

④ I am Godfrey of Lincolnshire. **Color** me grandly for battle and label me by writing all of the words from the chest next to the things they describe.

JOKE

Q: Why are police officers strong?

A: They can hold up a line of traffic with one hand.

YOUR TURN TO WRITE

> **TIP FOR TOP WRITERS!**
> When writing a narrative . . .
> - **Plan** your narrative (setting, problem, resolution).
> - **Sequence** the events (problem).
> - Then **write** the story.

① Claudia is writing a narrative about someone being lost in the woods. In the story, the day turned cold and wet, and her character, Mr. Ibrahim, lost his way in the mist. Write a setting that would suit Claudia's narrative.

_____

_____

_____

_____

_____

_____

_____

_____

② Johnny Imahera wants to write a story about a guitar competition in which his character, Jason Jackson, won an electric guitar. He has gotten as far as writing about Jason playing in the competition on a borrowed guitar. Write a resolution that would fit his narrative.

_____

_____

_____

_____

_____

_____

_____

_____

YOUR TURN TO WRITE (cont.)

③ Choose one of the following titles/topics and plan a narrative about it using the outline below.

a. The Waterslide Wars   **b.** Beating the Bully   **c.** The Duck Wins!

Setting _____

_____

_____

_____

_____

_____

Problem (sequenced events) _____

_____

_____

_____

_____

_____

_____

_____

_____

Resolution _____

_____

_____

_____

_____

_____

_____

④ On a separate sheet of paper, rewrite your narrative according to your above outline. Be sure to proofread your story before writing your final draft.

LESSON 3 — Writing Humorous Verse

Poems that are funny usually have a **regular rhythm** (beat) and a **regular pattern of rhyming words**. Limericks are a famous kind of humorous verse.

STRUCTURE

LANGUAGE

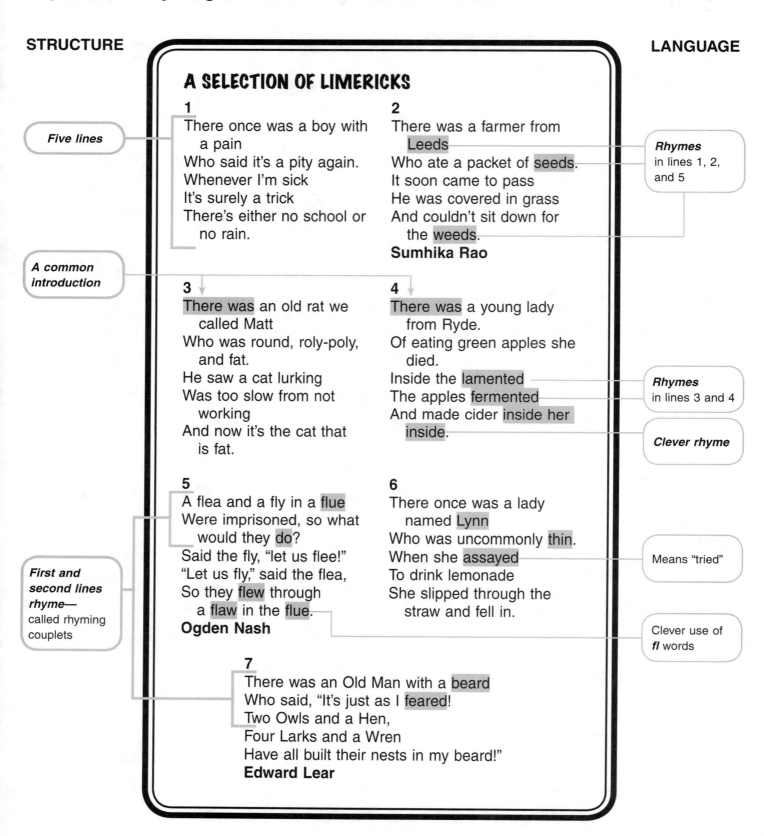

A SELECTION OF LIMERICKS

Five lines

1
There once was a boy with
    a pain
Who said it's a pity again.
Whenever I'm sick
It's surely a trick
There's either no school or
    no rain.

2
There was a farmer from
    Leeds
Who ate a packet of seeds.
It soon came to pass
He was covered in grass
And couldn't sit down for
    the weeds.
Sumhika Rao

Rhymes in lines 1, 2, and 5

A common introduction

3
There was an old rat we
    called Matt
Who was round, roly-poly,
    and fat.
He saw a cat lurking
Was too slow from not
    working
And now it's the cat that
    is fat.

4
There was a young lady
    from Ryde.
Of eating green apples she
    died.
Inside the lamented
The apples fermented
And made cider inside her
    inside.

Rhymes in lines 3 and 4

Clever rhyme

First and second lines rhyme— called rhyming couplets

5
A flea and a fly in a flue
Were imprisoned, so what
    would they do?
Said the fly, "let us flee!"
"Let us fly," said the flea,
So they flew through
    a flaw in the flue.
Ogden Nash

6
There once was a lady
    named Lynn
Who was uncommonly thin.
When she assayed
To drink lemonade
She slipped through the
    straw and fell in.

Means "tried"

Clever use of fl words

7
There was an Old Man with a beard
Who said, "It's just as I feared!
Two Owls and a Hen,
Four Larks and a Wren
Have all built their nests in my beard!"
Edward Lear

WHAT DID YOU READ?

① **Circle** the correct answer. The sick schoolboy feels . . .

    a. cheated   **b.** that life is unfair   **c.** both a and b

② **Explain** how you think the man from Leeds ended up unable to sit down "because of the weeds."

_____

_____

③ **Write** one sentence explaining what happened to Matt the rat.

_____

④ **Where** did the apple-eating girl live? _____

⑤ **Circle** the correct answer. The word *lamented* means:

    a. mourned for   **b.** very sick

⑥ **Write** the product you get when apples are fermented. _____

⑦ **Circle** the correct answer. The two trapped creatures in Ogden Nash's limerick are . . .

    a. a fly and a flue   **b.** a flea and a flaw

    c. a fly and a flea   **d.** a flaw and a flue

⑧ **Write** what happened to Lynn. _____

_____

⑨ **Complete** this sentence.

All the creatures that nested in the old man's beard were B ___ ___ ___ ___.

HOW IS IT WRITTEN?

① **Read** all the limericks carefully, then **complete** the following sentence:

The first line of a limerick always introduces the S ___ BJ ___ ___ T that the limerick is about.

② **Circle two** correct answers. The second line of a limerick tells us . . .

    a. what the subject of line 1 did or said

    b. something about the subject in line 1

    c. how old the subject in line 1 is

③ The first two lines and the last line of a limerick always **rhyme**. **Write** the rhyming words of lines 1, 2, and 5 in limerick 4.

_____   _____   _____

☀ SPELLING AND MEANING

Word Box	either	pain	flea	flaw	lament
	packet	wren	flee	flue	ferment
	lurking	could	flew	beard	lemonade

Be careful with **homophones** (words that sound the same but are spelled differently and have different meanings, such as **flee** and **flea**). **Check** your **dictionary** if you are not sure what a word means.

① Circle the right answer to these questions.

   a. Which one can bite you? **flee / flea**

   b. Which one allows smoke to escape a chimney? **flew / flue**

   c. Which one is a piece, section, or side of something? **pane / pain**

② The word **lurking** suggests a **bad** intention in someone waiting and watching. The cat in limerick 3 was watching Matt the rat with a very bad intention, wasn't he? **Circle** all the words in the following list that also suggest a **bad** intention:

   sneak   look   spy   watch   creep   tell   tattle   take   rob

③ **Insert** the correct words from the list in question 2 into these sentences. (You will not need all the words in the list.)

   a. Some beetles _____ very slowly over the ground.

   b. It is against the law to _____ people of their belongings.

   c. Dave had to _____ a candy bar out of the cupboard.

   d. I like to _____ the boats in the harbor.

④ **Insert** a word from the word box above to complete each sentence.

   a. A vintner will _____ grape juice to make wine.

   b. We will _____ go swimming or go fishing.

   c. The bruise from that fall is causing me a lot of _____.

   d. I got a sign-up _____ when I joined the soccer team.

   e. A cartoon pirate sometimes has red hair and a red _____.

⑤ The word **wren** begins with a **silent w**.

   These words all begin with a **silent w**. Can you **complete** them?

   a. a tool for undoing nuts and bolts: W ___ E ___ ___ H

   b. to twist the water out of wet clothes: W ___ ___ NG

   c. not right: W ___ ___ ___ ___

   d. to make marks on paper: W ___ ___ ___ E

   e. to move like a worm: W ___ ___ GG ___ ___

SPELLING AND MEANING (cont.)

⑥ **Draw lines** to match these **opposite** pairs.

a. black **or**	full
b. wet **or**	going
c. sunny **or**	white
d. coming **or**	dry
e. empty **or**	cloudy

GRAMMAR

Adjectives stand in **front of nouns**.

Example: There was a <u>young</u> (adjective) <u>lady</u> (noun) from Ryde.

Adjectives can also **follow verbs**.

Example: Ivan's tongue <u>turned</u> (verb) <u>red</u> (adjective) when he ate licorice.

Adjectives tell us **size**, **shape**, **color**, and **number**.

Examples: big, square, blue, four

Adjectives can also tell us **mood**, **personality**, and **special features**.

Examples: happy, mean, heavy

① **Circle** all the adjectives of color and shape in these sentences.

   a. Clowns are often tall and thin, have red noses, and wear baggy pants.

   b. Laurel was a skinny comedian who walked with bandy legs. Hardy, his partner, had the build of a round ball with two little feet under it and a round, black hat on top.

② **Circle** all the adjectives of mood and personality.

   a. Harry invited the lonely newcomer to join his jolly group of friends.

   b. Selfish people are never happy people.

   c. Mrs. Georgiou is a thoughtful woman. She is kind to everyone.

③ **Circle** all the adjectives that tell us about special features.

   a. Planets are visible but many stars are invisible to the naked eye.

   b. These apples are ripe, but the oranges are unripe.

   c. Taipans are venomous snakes, but green tree snakes are harmless.

PUNCTUATION

Sometimes we combine two words and **abbreviate** (shorten) them. We call these shortened words **contractions**. When we abbreviate, we insert an apostrophe (') in place of the missing letter or syllable.

Example: This **is not** my hat. → This **isn't** my hat.

Abbreviate the underlined words and **insert** an apostrophe in place of the missing letters.

① He <u>is not</u> a good comedian. People <u>do not</u> laugh at his jokes.

   _____   _____

② I <u>have not</u> laughed so much in a long time. <u>She is</u> a great comedian.

   _____   _____

☼ FUN WITH WORDS

① English is a funny language. Can you **complete** these sayings?

   a. If something is to my liking, I say it T __ CKL __ S my fancy.

   b. If I hit my elbow and squeal with pain, I wail that I hit my F __ NN __ bone.

   c. If I laugh until I cry, I say I laughed my H __ __ D off.

   d. If I feel dizzy, I say my head is SPI __ __ ING.

Lots of fun can be had by making up words. Lewis Carroll once wrote a poem called "The Jabberwocky." Two of its lines are:

'Twas brillig and the slithy toves

did gyre and gimble in the wabe.

Most of these words are made up, but somehow they seem to make sense because we recognize nouns and adjectives and verbs among them.

② Can you **answer** these questions?

   a. What were the *toves* doing? _____ ing and _____ ing (verbs)

   b. Where were they doing this? In the _____. (noun)

   c. What was the weather like? It was _____. (adjective)

   d. What were the *toves* like? They were _____. (adjective)

③ Now it is your turn. **Invent** words to name the following:

   a. One noun to name a small, furry animal shaped like a ball with no arms or legs and only one eye: _____

   b. Two verbs for the actions of this animal: _____ _____

   c. One adjective to describe the animal: _____

   d. One adjective to describe the hot sticky weather: _____

   e. One noun to name the green rain that is falling: _____

④ Using your new words, **complete** this sentence. Your new sentence will follow the pattern of "The Jabberwocky" sentence above.

   'Twas _____ and the _____ _____

   did _____ and _____ in the _____.

   Ask your friends what they picture in their minds when you read them your sentence.

⑤ These people all make their living out of being funny. Can you **name** them?

   a. __ __ __ __N   **b.** M__ __ __ __ __ __ __ __   **c.** V __ __ T __ __ L __ Q __ __ __ __

YOUR TURN TO WRITE

> **TIP FOR TOP WRITERS!**
> When you write a limerick, **check** its rhythm by **reading it aloud**. If the rhythm is regular, it will sound like this: *de da / de de da / de de da*
> *Example:*   There once / was a boy / with a pain
>   *de da / de de da / de de da*

① Can you complete the second line of this introduction to a limerick with a rhyming word?

There was an old man from Coonamble

Who loved to wander and R __ M __ LE

② Here are some limerick first lines. Can you add their second lines from the box below?

a. There once was a lady of fame _____

b. There once was a miner named Pyner _____

c. There was an old man from Japan _____

> Who sported an awful black shiner
>
> Who only ate water with bran
>
> Who couldn't remember her name

③ Here are some first lines for limericks. Can you write a second line for each one? Remember that the last words of each line must rhyme.

a. There was an old man in the hills   **b.** There once was a witch with a cat

_____   _____

c. There once was a painter named Jim   **d.** There was a green frog in a bog

_____   _____

④ Now that you have the idea, write your own limerick. You may choose one of the first lines above to start your limerick. Remember to write exactly five lines.

_____

_____

_____

_____

_____

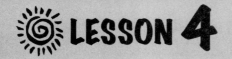

You write a **report** to **inform** your reader. It is a **factual**, not an imaginative, piece of writing.

STRUCTURE

- **Introduction**
  statement followed by explanation

- **Body of report**
  (in groups of facts)

- Autumn work

- Hives

- Chambers and workers

- Queens and drones

- Young bees and growing up

LANGUAGE

- **Adjective**
  introduces idea of bees being interesting

- **Technical words**

- **Short factual statements**

- **Clear, informative verbs**

- **Technical words**

- **Only absolutely necessary adjectives**
  used in a report

BEES

Bees are very strange creatures. They have their own way of telling each other that they have found a new flower. They bring some of its nectar back to the hive and then do a little dance that shows where the flower is and how far away it is.

In autumn, the worker bees go out and collect as much nectar and pollen as they can carry. Then they return to make honey and store it for the long, cold winter.

Bees build hives, but their hives are not always dome-shaped like people draw them in storybooks. They are usually five stories high. The queen bee always has the bottom story. In between the bottom story and all the rest there are bars only just wide enough for the workers to squeeze through. The queen bee can never go up to the other floors because she is bigger than all the other bees.

The stories the queen can't enter are where the store chambers are. There are chambers for pollen and nectar and royal jelly. If there is a fire, the workers have to seal the walls and entrance of the chambers. They have to move the honey and the nectar and pollen away from the hot walls of the chamber.

The queen bee is the only bee that can lay eggs. She mates with a male bee called a *drone*. Once the queen has laid the eggs, she throws the drone out because a drone just sits around eating honey and nectar. He cannot go out and collect pollen because drones do not have pollen-carrying sacs on their legs like the workers have.

Young bees are called *nurses* because they have to nurse the newborn bees whether they like it or not. What a bee ends up being when it grows up depends on what it eats. If it is to be a queen, it must feed on royal jellies and it must never, ever set eyes on another queen. If it does, they must fight until only one of them is still alive.

Penny (age 9)

WHAT DID YOU READ?

① **Circle** the correct answer.

Bees communicate the location of a new flower by **action / sound**.

② **Name** two activities that keep bees busy in autumn.

a. _____

b. _____

③ **Circle** the correct answer.

The queen bee occupies a chamber in the middle of the hive. **True / False**

④ **Explain** why the queen is unable to move between the floors of the hive.

_____

⑤ **Circle** the correct answer.

Drones / Nurses are the bees that look after the newborn bees.

⑥ **Circle** the correct answer. A *sac* is a . . .

a. small basket carried by bees   b. tiny pocket on the leg of a bee

c. spelling mistake

⑦ **Complete** this sentence.

What a young bee grows up to be depends on _____ .

HOW IS IT WRITTEN?

① A report contains facts. **Name** two facts you find in the thrid paragraph.

_____

_____

② A report uses technical words. **Write** down three technical words you find in the report.

_____   _____   _____

③ A report usually does not include opinions, only facts. It is usually written in the third person (he, she, it, they).

Circle the **two** sentences that would **not** appear in a report.

a. I like insects.   b. Insects come in all sizes and shapes.

c. Insects have six legs.   d. I think insects are funny.

④ **Complete** the following:

Adjectives in reports usually tell us SH ____ PE, C ____ LOR, S ____ ZE, and

N ____ MB ____ R.

SPELLING AND MEANING

Word Box	collect	story	chamber	communicate
	pollen	creature	entrance	strange
	nectar	squeeze	laid	dome

Pay special attention to **double-letters** and to **final syllables** when you are learning spelling and don't forget the **look, cover, write, and check** method of learning to spell (see page 8).

① **Insert** a word from the word box to complete each sentence.

a. Birds _____ straw and twigs to build their nests.

b. _____ is found at the center of a flower.

c. Humpback whales _____ by singing to each other.

d. _____ to the zoo costs five dollars for children.

e. An igloo is a _____-shaped house built of ice.

Not all plurals (more than one) end in **–s**. Some have different endings, some are different words altogether, and some words don't change at all.

Examples: bee → bees, mouse → mice, sheep → sheep

② **Write** the plural of each of the following animals.

a. horse _____   **b.** fish _____

c. pig _____   **d.** cow _____

e. goose _____   **f.** koala _____

③ **Write** the plurals of these nouns.

a. creature _____   **b.** story _____

c. burrow _____   **d.** hive _____

e. hatchery _____   **f.** hutch _____

Words that sound the same but are spelled differently are called **homophones**.

Example: **cent** (one-hundredth of a dollar) and **scent** (an aroma)

④ **Draw a line** from each homophone to its right meaning.

a. bore   relating to a wedding

b. boar   passenger boat

c. bridle   male pig

d. bridal   equipment used to control a horse

e. ferry   tiny mythical creature with wings

f. fairy   to cause to feel boredom

GRAMMAR

Careful choice of **verbs** is very important in a report. A verb is a word that tells us about **doing**, **being**, **saying**, **having**, and **the use of all our senses**.

Examples: Jim **cuts** the paper in half. (doing verb)

   All the bees **are** in the hive. (being verb)

   Dogs **hear** sounds unheard by us. (sensing verb)

① **Circle** all the verbs in these sentences:

   a. Owls hunt at night.

   b. Snakes hibernate in winter.

   c. Ants are very intelligent insects.

   d. An eclipse of the sun is a rare event.

   e. Eagles watch the ground from high in the air.

② Sometimes a verb contains more than one word (e.g., Fruit bats **are hanging** upside down in the mango tree.). **Circle** the **complete verbs** in these sentences.

   a. The little, brown geckoes were sunning themselves on a rock.

   b. A mob of kangaroos is resting in the shade.

   c. Three lions were hunting an antelope.

   d. A blue whale was cruising close to the ice pack.

③ **Complete** the sentences below by inserting a verb made from the underlined adjective from the first sentence. The first is done for you.

   a. Swallows are <u>migratory</u> birds.

   Swallows **migrate** between China and Australia.

   b. Bears are <u>hibernating</u> animals.

   Bears ___ ___ ___ ___ ___ ___ ___ ___ ___ in caves during winter.

   c. Cattle gather in <u>defensive</u> herds.

   Cattle gather in herds to ___ ___ ___ ___ ___ ___ themselves.

PUNCTUATION

When we write lists (of things or of activities) we **separate** the items in the list with a comma (,).

   Example: Susie packed sunscreen, sunglasses, a towel, a sandwich, and a drink for the beach.

Insert all of the missing commas:

a.   Ants stand guard hunt trap build climb and migrate.

b.   Pandas are known for sleeping eating and sleeping again.

c.   Dolphins are famed for diving leaping out of the water barrelling and somersaulting.

FUN WITH WORDS

① Animal babies have special names (e.g., a baby cow is a *calf*). Can you **name** these animal babies? Use your dictionary to help you.

a. A baby bird is a NE __ __ LING.

b. A baby elephant is a C A __ F.

c. A baby lion is a C __ __.

d. A baby fish is a FING __ __ LING.

e. A baby whale is a C __ LF.

f. A baby swan is a CY __ __ __ T.

② Some creatures are only **active at night**. We call them **nocturnal** creatures. **Find** all the nocturnal creatures in this cage and release them into the night by writing their names among the moon and stars.

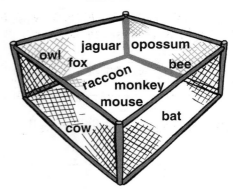

③ Most animal homes have special names. With the help of your dictionary can you **name** these homes?

a. an eagle's nest: EYR __ __

b. a maze of connected rabbit burrows: WA __ R __ N

c. a turkey's nest: MOU __ D

d. a wild dog's hole or cave: LA __ R

YOUR TURN TO WRITE

> TIP FOR TOP WRITERS!
>
> When you **write** a report make sure you . . .
> - only write facts
> - choose precise verbs
> - use technical words where needed
> - use only factual adjectives

YOUR TURN TO WRITE (cont.)

Using the facts in the box below and an encyclopedia, **outline** a report on the giant anaconda on the lines that follow. Then **write** your final report on a separate sheet of paper.

THE GIANT ANACONDA

- water snake
- found in tropical rivers (South America)
- so-called because of size: average length 16 feet, and some longer
- heavily built
- dark green with large, oval black spots

- prey: small animals, birds, other reptiles
- lies in wait in water
- kills by constriction: wraps prey in coils and crushes it
- nests in leaf litter on jungle floor
- can produce up to 75 young at one time
- hunts at night

Identification and location _____

_____

_____

Appearance _____

_____

_____

_____

Nest and young _____

_____

_____

_____

Prey _____

_____

Hunting habits _____

_____

_____

_____

Conclusion _____

_____

_____

LESSON 5 — Writing a Description of a Place

A **description** of a place usually occurs inside a longer text (e.g., a narrative or a recount). When we **describe** a place, we aim to make that place real to the reader so that the reader can picture it in his or her mind.

STRUCTURE

- Introduction
- Body of description
- Outside appearance
- First impressions
- The floor
- The shelves
- Conclusion
- Comment

GRANDFATHER'S OLD SHED

Down at the back of Grandfather's place there is a very old wooden shed. It might have been painted green once, but now it's mostly gray wood, with just a few peeling patches of green on the door.

It has a crooked door and a crooked roof. Even its walls are crooked. It leans towards the fence as if it's been pushed. Maybe the wind pushed it for years and years until it just got tired of standing up straight.

The day I got to see inside the shed was a wet day. By mid-morning I had nothing to do. Grandfather, who doesn't like people standing around idle, gave me an umbrella and sent me down to the shed.

"Have a look around and see if you can find me a long weight," he told me with a wink. "It might take you a while."

I ran down to the shed happily, pushed the door open, and sneezed. Dust fell all over me. There was dust everywhere. Cobwebs hung in corners and around the shelves that lined the walls. It was dark and very dusty, but it smelled nice: a bit like sunshine and grease and chopped wood all mixed together.

Odd lengths of timber, some pieces of guttering, and a wooden ladder lay across the rafters over my head. There was nothing like a long weight up there. I began to turn through the boxes stacked up on the floor among wood shavings from long ago. Some held old-fashioned tools and pieces of coiled wire, others held dusty old bottles that I think were preserving jars, and one box was full of really old Donald Duck comics. I told myself I would come back here later and read them all.

I stood up and looked along the shelves. There were two funny old lamps with glass tops and round, metal tanks with wicks in them. Farther on, I found a row of bottles in all sorts of shapes and sizes and they were all blue.

Blue glass was something I had not seen before. I took one of the bottles over to the window to look at it properly. When I rubbed the dust off it and held it up to the light, the sun suddenly came out. Shining through the bottle glass, it threw a lovely blue light over my hands.

When I went back to the house I told Grandfather I couldn't find a long weight but that I'd found this beautiful blue bottle. He laughed and washed the bottle for me, saying I could keep it.

Then he said, "There are two ways of spelling 'weight,' you know." I am still thinking about that one.

Andrew (age 9)

LANGUAGE

- Good detail
- **Repetition** emphasizes age
- Good choice of adjective
- Details of sight and smell
- Interesting details
- **Place words** to make different position clear
- **Joke** — a homophone joke

WHAT DID YOU READ?

① **Circle** the correct answer. The shed is made of . . .

    a. iron   **b.** aluminum   **c.** wood

② **Circle** the **two** correct answers. The shed is crooked because . . .

    a. it's old   **b.** perhaps the wind pushed it

    c. it was built that way   **d.** it's missing part of a wall

③ When the writer entered the shed, **what two things** immediately confirm that it is very old?

    _____   _____

④ **What** does the writer say about the smell of the shed?

    _____

⑤ **What** is the other spelling of *weight*? _____

⑥ Why does the writer's grandfather really send him to the shed?

    _____

    _____

HOW IS IT WRITTEN?

① **Circle** the most correct and specific answer. Where do we first read about the shed?

    a. in the first paragraph   **b.** in the first sentence   **c.** in the fourth paragraph

② The writer uses his sense of sight to show us what he sees in the shed. What other senses does he use? **Circle** all the correct answers.

    a. taste   **b.** touch   **c.** smell   **d.** hearing

③ **Circle** the correct answer. When describing the interior of the shed, the writer . . .

    a. mentions the structure of the shed (floor, walls, window, and rafters)

    b. mentions the contents of the shed

    c. both of the above

④ **Circle** two correct answers. The writer describes the contents of the shed because . . .

    a. they are part of what is fascinating about the shed

    b. there's not much you can write about an old shed

    c. they explain what the shed is used for

⑤ **Complete** this sentence.

    A place description requires the careful choice of AD ___ ___ ___ T ___ VES.

☼ SPELLING AND MEANING

Word Box	crooked	weight	label	towards
	straight	wait	laugh	idle
	umbrella	grease	wooden	sneeze

When you spell, say the word aloud and clearly. Then learn to spell it. For example, many people have trouble spelling **umbrella** because they do not say it correctly. It only has three syllables **um/brel/la**.

① **Insert** a word from the word box to complete each sentence.

    a. Please draw a _____ line margin down the page.

    b. The carrier struggled under the _____ of his load.

    c. The _____ on the bottle warned: Poison! Dangerous!

    d. All the traffic stood _____ while police removed the wrecked vehicles.

    e. People cough and _____ with the common cold.

② Some words can be used as both a **verb** and a **noun**. **Find** one in the word box and **insert** it in this sentence two times.

    Please ___ ___ ___ ___ ___ ___ the hinges on the shed door to stop it from

    squeaking, but don't get ___ ___ ___ ___ ___ ___ on your jeans.

③ **Choose** the correct homophone from the box below to insert in the following sentences.

wait	reeds	pale	peel	reel	weight	reads	pail	peal	real

    a. Cold, driving rain and a bitter wind made the long ___ ___ ___ ___ seem endless.
    b. A ___ ___ ___ ___ of bells drifted across the valley in the stillness of the evening.
    c. The sound was the rustle of ducks among the ___ ___ ___ ___ ___ beside the river.
    d. Beside the tackle box stood a brand new rod and ___ ___ ___ ___.
    e. In the corner of the shed stood an old dairy ___ ___ ___ ___ for carrying milk.
    f. Among the coins in the dusty chest was a ___ ___ ___ ___ gold dollar.
    g. The faded paint on the old fence was beginning to ___ ___ ___ ___.

④ Words that are opposite in meaning are called **antonyms**. **Draw lines** from the words in the first column to their antonyms in the second column.

    a. straight   busy

    b. laugh   open

    c. idle   crooked

    d. build   cry

    e. close   demolish

GRAMMAR

Compound sentences have two equally important parts. Each contains a subject and a verb, and both parts are joined by a **comma**, followed by the word ***and***, ***but***, or ***or***.

Examples: Julie <u>will play</u> (verb) the flute, ***and*** Wafa <u>will play</u> (verb) the saxophone.

Kang <u>will play</u> (verb) the drums, ***or*** he <u>will play</u> (verb) violin at the concert.

Complex sentences have **one important part** (principal clause) and one **less important part** (subordinate clause). Both parts contain verbs and both parts are joined by a comma and a joining word (conjunction). In this example, the subordinate clause is underlined.

Example: The house **is** (verb) in good condition, ***<u>although</u>*** <u>(joining word) it</u> **<u>needs</u>** <u>(verb) some new paint</u>.

① **Name** these sentences as **compound** or **complex** in the space provided.

   a. If you have too many boxes, you can store them in our garage. _____

   b. We store paint in the shed, and we store timber across its rafters. _____

   c. John can clean the shelves, or help Peter wash the windows. _____

   d. Because the house is abandoned, it will be demolished. _____

② **Underline** all the principal clauses and **circle** all the subordinate clauses.

   a. Unless there is a breeze, the paint won't dry.

   b. While we were in the old shed, we saw a redback spider.

   c. Even though there were cobwebs in the attic, we were not frightened.

③ **Make** one sentence out of each of these sentence pairs by using joining words such as ***though***, ***although***, ***if***, ***unless***, ***while***, and ***when*** at the beginning of each.

   a. It is raining. I will go to the bakery. _____

   b. It is so old. The school still has not fallen down. _____

   c. You are here. We will paint the fence. _____

PUNCTUATION

Quotation marks (" ") enclose the exact words someone says.

Example: "Have a look around and see if you can find me a long weight," he said.

① **Insert** all necessary quotation marks.

   a.   Does dust make you sneeze? Ibrahim asked Paul.

   b.   Hand me some more nails, the carpenter told his apprentice.

If the actual words spoken are broken by other words, **enclose only the words spoken in quotation marks**.

Example: "I've dropped these," he sighed. "Pass me some more screws, please."

② **Insert** all necessary quotation marks.

   a.   Help! he shouted. The wind is lifting the roof off!

   b.   I know you like the beach, said Melissa, but I prefer the mountains.

FUN WITH WORDS

① In his grandfather's shed, the writer found all sorts of things. Here they are in scrambled form. Can you **unscramble** them? The first letter has been placed for you.

a. TTOBLES   B_____

b. MOCCIS   C_____

c. SPLAM   L_____

d. LOOTS   T_____

② The following are all words naming buildings. **Choose** the correct one for each illustration.

observatory   skyscraper   cottage   cathedral   igloo   lighthouse   mosque

a. _____   **b.** _____   **c.** _____   **d.** _____

③ People have used tools for many years. Can you **name** the hand tools for these tasks?

a. fixing nails: H ___ ___ M ___ R   **b.** cutting wood: S ___ ___

c. carving wood: CH ___ S ___ L   **d.** fixing nuts and bolts: W ___ ___ N ___ H

e. fixing screws: S___ ___ ___ ___ DR ___ ___ ___ R

④ **Follow** these instructions using metric measurements:

a. Cut a length of string 2 meters 25 centimeters long.

b. Use the top 10 centimeters to **tie** the string to the **middle** of a pencil.

c. Tie a knot in the string every 50 centimeters down from the pencil.

d. Use the 15 or so centimeters left to **tie** to a small, heavy weight
(e.g., a small piece of heavy wood or a small stone).

e. Now you have made a measuring tool. You can use it to **measure** how deep
something is or how high it is. **Hold** the pencil level and just drop the weight to the
bottom of what you want to measure. When the string is still, count the knots in the
string to the top of what you are measuring. Then you multiply the number of knots by
50 centimeters and you have your measurement.

⑤ To name the tool you have just made, **answer** the questions below, then combine them.

a. Small fruit with reddish-purple skin: P ___ ___ ___

b. Short for "Robert": ___ ___ ___

This tool, used for thousands of years, is called a P ___ ___ ___ B ___ ___ ___

☀ YOUR TURN TO WRITE

> **TIP FOR TOP WRITERS!**
> When describing a place, first **tell** where it is and then **tell** all about it, including what you **see**, **hear**, **smell**, **feel**, and **think** about it.

① Stand in the doorway of your kitchen and look at it carefully. Ask these questions.

   a. Where is the kitchen in my house? Who uses this kitchen?

   b. What happens in this kitchen? (Don't just think about cooking.)

   c. How is it laid out? What is the busiest part? Why is that so?

   d. Is it more or less important than other parts of the house? Why?

   e. What can I see and what can I smell in this kitchen? Is it always the same?

   f. Is there anything I really like or dislike in this kitchen? (Think about colors, sounds, smells, shapes, chores, routines, and so on.)

② Using your answers to the questions, write a description of the kitchen in your house. Use the space below to outline your description, then write your final draft on a separate sheet of paper.

Introduction _____

_____

_____

Paragraph 2 (What happens in the kitchen?) _____

_____

_____

Paragraph 3 (People in the kitchen) _____

_____

_____

Paragraph 4 (What's special about our kitchen?) _____

_____

_____

_____

Comment (What I think/feel about our kitchen.) _____

_____

An **opinion speech** states an argument, argues it strongly, and concludes by restating the argument and inviting the audience to agree.

STRUCTURE

LANGUAGE

Address
(to audience)

Statement
of argument

Body of case
(evidence to support argument)

Conclusion

TELEVISION'S NEGATIVE INFLUENCE

Good morning, Fourth Grade.

I believe television influences our community in a negative way. Television influences people to copy what they see. Programs and advertising both influence people to copy what they see. They buy products because they see them on TV. They talk and act the way the characters on their favorite shows do. This is definitely a case of TV having a negative influence on people.

TV advertisements influence the way people buy things. Advertisements intrigue them with their bright colors and loud music. Advertisers only tell you good things about a product and not the bad things, so people are persuaded to buy things they don't need. Sometimes they buy worthless things or things that break. Television advertising encourages people to waste money.

When people watch the same show on TV a number of times, they start to pick up the habits of characters on the show. Some of these habits are extremely bad, like laziness, bad attitudes, and even swearing and hurting.

Children see lots of violence on TV, real violence and cartoon violence. A survey carried out by the International Coalition Against Violence showed that many cartoons are violent. *Bugs Bunny* and *Road Runner* show an average of 55 violent acts every hour. The News every night is full of violence, too. That is worse because it's real violence, while in cartoons it's just pretend.

Dr. Patricia Edgar, director of the Australian Children's Television Foundation, says, "Children are more afraid of what they see on the news than on other shows because they know it is real." I think she is right and that this is not good for children. Television should not show violence to frighten us. Children need to learn to be friends. We should not learn about violence.

Television definitely has a very negative influence on our community. We should all be very worried about it.

Stephanie (age 9)

All definite statements
(no "I think")

Good choice of verbs

Examples
explain statement

Quotations
from authorities make your case believable

Statements everyone can agree with
to win approval of audience

Audience included
in statement

✺ WHAT DID YOU READ?

① **Who** is the audience listening to this speech? _____

② **What** is it that catches people's attention about advertisements?

    a. _____   **b.** _____

③ **Name** two bad habits the speaker believes TV watchers can pick up.

    a. _____   **b.** _____

④ **Circle** the correct answer: **True** or **False**

    Dr. Patricia Edgar is the director of the International Coalition Against Violence.

⑤ The speaker considers TV a negative influence for several reasons. **Circle** the reason she **does not** mention.

    a. People copy bad habits.

    b. People buy worthless things.

    c. People waste money on things they don't need.

    d. There are too many crime shows on TV.

    e. There is a lot of violence on TV.

✺ HOW IS IT WRITTEN?

① **What** words in the first sentence tell us that this is an **opinion** speech? _____

② **Circle** the most correct and specific answer. The writer's opinion first appears in . . .

    a. the first paragraph   **b.** the first sentence   **c.** the last sentence

③ **Circle** the correct answer. The writer's opinion is restated in . . .

    a. the middle of the speech   **b.** the last paragraph   **c.** the second-to-last paragraph

④ To persuade others to share your opinion, it helps to include facts to support what you say. **Write** down one fact you find in the fourth paragraph.

    _____

    _____

⑤ An opinion is always more believable if supported by someone in authority. This speaker quotes two authorities. **Name** one of them.

    _____

⑥ When persuading an audience to agree with your opinion, it is helpful to include them in your speech. **Circle** the words below that **include** the audience. (They are all in the last two paragraphs.)

    a. us   **b.** violence   **c.** our   **d.** influence   **e.** we

☼ SPELLING AND MEANING

Word Box	television	positive	extremely	waste
	influence	negative	attitude	money
	community	advertisement	international	product

Sometimes it helps to recognize the meaning of **prefixes** (first syllables) when you are learning to spell (e.g., the prefix *tele–*, which means *far* or *at a distance*, and the prefix *inter–*, which means *between*). Then you only have to learn the rest of the word.

① Remembering that the prefix *inter–* means *between*, **match** these words to their meanings.

a. interrupt	between states
b. international	come between two quarrelling people
c. interstate	get in the way of someone's work
d. intersection	between countries
e. intervene	point where two roads meet
f. interfere	break into a conversation

② **Label** these pictures with a *tele–* word.

a. _____   b. _____   c. _____ pole

③ **Insert** a word from the word box above to complete these sentences.

a. Our street is a little _____ of friends and neighbors.

b. Rain will have a bad _____ on the way a horse gallops.

c. The positive effect of rain is garden growth; the _____ effect is the cancellation of our picnic.

d. It is _____ cold in Chicago today at 15 degrees Fahrenheit.

e. The Olympic Games is an _____ sports gathering.

✺ GRAMMAR

Adverbs tell us things about a verb. They tell us **how**, **when**, and **where** an action happens.

    Examples: Regina reads <u>well</u>. (adverb, how)

                 Omar was sick <u>yesterday</u>. (adverb, when)

                 The cat sleeps <u>there</u>. (adverb, where)

Adverbs also tell us about adjectives. They tell us to what **degree** the adjective is true.

    Examples: I am <u>very</u> excited about going on holidays.

                 Peter only injured himself <u>slightly</u> when he fell.

Many adverbs end in *–ly*.

    Examples: finally, hungrily, usually, rarely

① **Circle** the **adverbs** in these sentences.

    a. Television advertisements for toys are shown early in the day.

    b. Jodie watches nature programs eagerly.

    c. Video game systems are usually very expensive.

    d. Game shows are common on television because they can be made cheaply.

    e. Young viewers react positively to comedies and cartoons.

② **Circle** the **adverbs** in these sentences and **write** *how*, *when*, or *where* in the space provided to show what the adverb tells us.

    a. Mr. Sung is advertising a sale today. _____

    b. News reports usually occur between 6 and 7 P.M. _____

    c. Television cameras were there to capture the race. _____

    d. Many television shows are watched internationally. _____

    e. Some advertising influences people negatively. _____

✺ PUNCTUATION

Most writing is arranged in **paragraphs**—**one idea** per paragraph, **one event** per paragraph, **one speaker** per paragraph. **Read** the following opinion carefully, and then use a **paragraph sign** (¶) to **mark** where each new paragraph should begin.

I firmly believe that if you have a pet, you should look after it as if it is a member of your family. After all, it lives in the same house as you and shares every part of your life, probably even more closely than your friends do. So what does looking after your pet like a member of your family mean? First, it means your pet is fed daily. It means it is fed what is right for its breed, not just scraps from the kitchen. It means you make sure it has plenty of clean water to drink every day. Like us, pets feel the heat and the cold. In winter you must make sure it has a warm, dry shelter out of the wind and rain, and in summer you must see that it has lots of cool shade to protect it from the heat. If it is sick, you take it to the vet; and if it is miserable, you play with it and reassure it that it is your friend. We owe our pets the same loyal friendship they give us.

☼ FUN WITH WORDS

① Television studios make many different kinds of programs. Here are the names of some of them. Can you **match** the word to the program it names?

a. animation	competition with competitors and prizes
b. drama	how to improve your life, house, garden, etc.
c. current affairs	story in cartoon format
d. lifestyle	serious, acted story about people and events
e. comedy	program discussing real events and issues
f. game show	program designed to make you laugh

② Communities are groups of living creatures who live together. Below are names of human communities. **Number** them in order from smallest to largest.

metropolis ____   city ____   village ____   town ____

③ These people are all happy, but some are happier than others. Using the adverbs **very**, **quite**, and **extremely**, **label** them according to their degree of happiness.

a. _____   **b.** _____   **c.** _____

④ When you give a speech, you must first **address** your audience. **Match** these terms of address to their audiences.

a. Ladies and Gentlemen	a judge
b. Mr. President	a minister named Smith
c. Fellow Football Players	a group of adults
d. Your Honor	the president
e. Reverend Smith	your football team

☼ YOUR TURN TO WRITE

> **TIP FOR TOP WRITERS!**
> In an opinion speech . . .
> - **Start** with an address/greeting to the audience.
> - **State** your opinion.
> - **Explain** and argue your opinion.
> - **Use** facts and quotations to **support** your opinion.
> - **End** by restating your opinion and asking the audience to agree.

① Make a list of the arguments you could use to support the opinion that everyone should play a sport.

a. _____

b. _____

c. _____

d. _____

② Write a statement of opinion to introduce the arguments you have written in question 1.

_____

_____

_____

_____

_____

_____

③ Re-read your answers to questions 1 and 2 and then write a conclusion to this expression of your opinion.

_____

_____

_____

_____

_____

④ Now rewrite your final speech on a separate sheet of paper.

Explaining what happens is a special kind of writing. It is always written in the **present tense**, and it is always **factual**. Double check your facts by doing some **research** before writing an explanation.

STRUCTURE

LANGUAGE

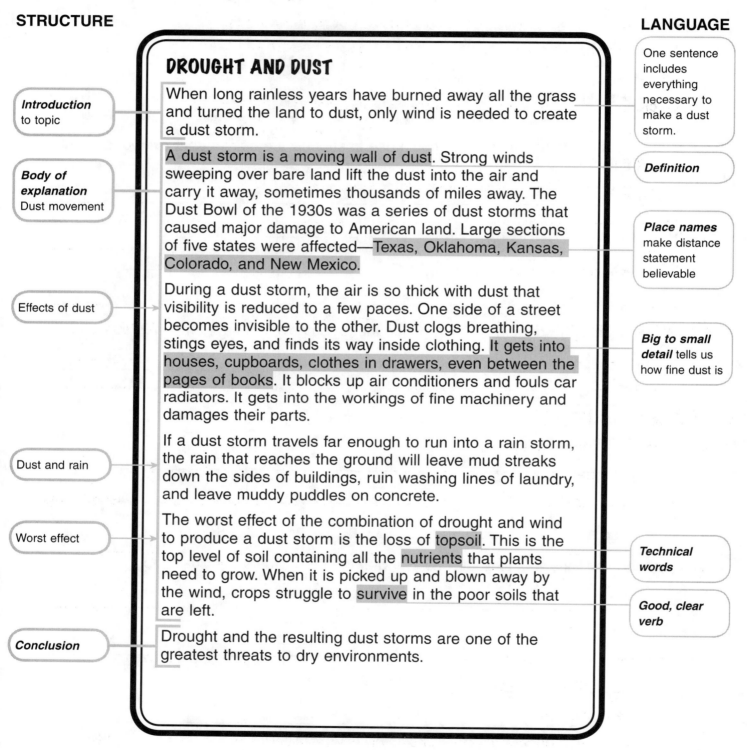

Introduction to topic

Body of explanation Dust movement

Effects of dust

Dust and rain

Worst effect

Conclusion

DROUGHT AND DUST

When long rainless years have burned away all the grass and turned the land to dust, only wind is needed to create a dust storm.

A dust storm is a moving wall of dust. Strong winds sweeping over bare land lift the dust into the air and carry it away, sometimes thousands of miles away. The Dust Bowl of the 1930s was a series of dust storms that caused major damage to American land. Large sections of five states were affected—Texas, Oklahoma, Kansas, Colorado, and New Mexico.

During a dust storm, the air is so thick with dust that visibility is reduced to a few paces. One side of a street becomes invisible to the other. Dust clogs breathing, stings eyes, and finds its way inside clothing. It gets into houses, cupboards, clothes in drawers, even between the pages of books. It blocks up air conditioners and fouls car radiators. It gets into the workings of fine machinery and damages their parts.

If a dust storm travels far enough to run into a rain storm, the rain that reaches the ground will leave mud streaks down the sides of buildings, ruin washing lines of laundry, and leave muddy puddles on concrete.

The worst effect of the combination of drought and wind to produce a dust storm is the loss of topsoil. This is the top level of soil containing all the nutrients that plants need to grow. When it is picked up and blown away by the wind, crops struggle to survive in the poor soils that are left.

Drought and the resulting dust storms are one of the greatest threats to dry environments.

One sentence includes everything necessary to make a dust storm.

Definition

Place names make distance statement believable

Big to small detail tells us how fine dust is

Technical words

Good, clear verb

☀ WHAT DID YOU READ?

① Drought makes a dust storm possible. **Circle** the answer that indicates what actually **starts** a dust storm.

    a. farmers   **b.** wind   **c.** lack of rain   **d.** bare ground

② **Circle** the correct answer. The Dust Bowl primarily affected . . .

    a. 5 states   **b.** 7 states   **c.** 4 states

③ **Circle** the correct answer. When a dust storm meets a rain storm . . .

    a. the rain dries up   **b.** the dust storm stops

    c. the rain is turned to muddy water

④ **List** two ways in which dust storms affect people personally.

    a. _____

    b. _____

⑤ **How** does dust affect fine machinery?

    _____

⑥ **Explain** why crops would struggle to survive in the year following a dust storm.

    _____

    _____

☀ HOW IS IT WRITTEN?

① **Circle** the correct answer.

    We learn what causes a dust storm in the first paragraph. **True / False**

② A good explanation includes a definition. **Write** the definition of a dust storm used in this text.

    _____

③ **What fact** does the writer include to prove that dust storms can travel far?

    _____

④ **Complete** this statement.

    The writer shows how dust can get into tiny spaces by listing spaces from

    L ___ ___ GEST to SM ___ ___ ___ EST.

⑤ **Complete** this sentence.

    The explanation ends with an emphasis on how serious a PR ___ B ___ ___ M a dust storm really is.

✹ SPELLING AND MEANING

Word Box	drought	visible	move	travel
	create	visibility	moving	traveled
	color	sometimes	bare	traveler

For verbs that end in **e**, drop the **e** when you add **ing** (e.g., move/moving).

① **Insert** the correct form of the verb in parentheses.

a. The camel train was _____ (travel) towards an oasis.

b. We are _____ (move) to Idaho for two years.

c. This experiment is _____ (prove) that water is made of oxygen and hydrogen.

d. My brother is _____ (label) his baseball gear.

e. We are still _____ (decide) whether to go to the movies.

② **Match** these words from the word box to their meanings.

a. drought
b. create
c. sometimes
d. bare

make
occasionally
without covering
a long time without rain

③ Sometimes we can make **antonyms** (words that mean the opposite) by adding a **prefix** (beginning syllable). **Make** antonyms of these words by adding the prefix **in–**.

a. visible (able to be seen) _____

b. audible (able to be heard) _____

c. tangible (able to be touched) _____

④ Using your answers from question 3, **substitute** one word for the phrase in parentheses.

a. In all the noise of the wind and thunder, the ring of the telephone was

_____ (could not be heard).

b. The mountain top was _____ (could not be seen) because of the low cloud.

c. The scent of flowers is an _____ (cannot be touched) delight.

🌀 SPELLING AND MEANING (cont.)

⑤ Some common **homophones** (same sound, different spelling) can cause confusion. **Complete** these sentences using the pictures to help you.

a.    **b.**    **c.**    **d.**

a. Please don't _____ on the wall.   **b.** The open drawer is _____ there.

c. There's a _____ in there.   **d.** The cupboard was _____.

🌀 GRAMMAR—ADVERB REVISION

① **Circle** the adverbs of degree in these sentences.

   a. He was absolutely amazed at his first sight of the dust storm.

   b. I know all about cyclones, but I am less certain about dust storms.

   c. Sue is very confident of completing her weather project on time.

② **Circle** all the adverbs of time, degree, and manner (how) in the following sentences.

   a. The kite danced wildly at the end of its string in the high wind.

   b. Tomorrow we will go on our excursion to the weather bureau.

   c. Keisha was very frightened when the dust made it hard to breathe.

🌀 PUNCTUATION

We already know an **apostrophe** (') shows us where a letter has been left out (e.g., is not → isn't, has not → hasn't).

An apostrophe also shows us that **someone owns something** (e.g., <u>Will's</u> soccer cleats, <u>Selena's</u> hockey stick).

① **Insert** an apostrophe where necessary.

   a. a farmers worst nightmare   **b.** a plants survival

   c. a students favorite subject   **d.** a meteorologists job

If a plural noun (more than one) owns something, the apostrophe is placed **after** the final *s* of that noun.

   Example: All the local farmer**s'** topsoil was swept away by the winds.

If the plural word does not end in *s*, then the apostrophe and *s* come at the end of the word.

   Example: The children**'s** shoes were all wet from the rain.

② **Insert** an apostrophe where necessary.

   a. High winds can damage birds wing feathers.

   b. Horses hooves can be badly cracked by dry, stony ground.

   c. Farmers crops need plenty of water and sunlight.

☀ FUN WITH WORDS

① These are all words meaning **dry**. Can you **unscramble** them?

a. IDAR → A ___ ___ D

b. RRENBA → B ___ ___ ___ ___ N

c. STYDU → D ___ ___ ___Y

d. TRHIYST → T ___ ___ ___ ___ ___Y

② This field has been in drought for two years. Fill it up with all the words you can think of that are related to **drought**. Think about temperature, plants, animals, and soil. One word has already been added.

barren

③ The most waterless areas of the world are called *deserts*. The things below are all found in deserts. Do you know what they are?

a. four-legged animal sometimes called the ship of the desert: C ___ ___ ___ L

b. tiny green place in the desert with water and palm trees: O ___ S ___ S

c. small brown fruit of the desert palm tree: D ___ T ___

④ Dust storms are one kind of storm. There are many other kinds of storms. Can you **name** them?

a. ___ ___ ___ ___ ___ CANE (think of moving faster so you won't be late)

b. ___ ___ ___ ___ ONE (think of the word *bicycle* losing some letters)

c. ___ ___ ___ ___ ADO (think of a word meaning *ripped*)

d. ___ ___ ___ ___ (think of a homonym for *Gail*)

e. TYPH ___ ___ ___ (think of the last three letters in the object that revolves around Earth)

f. TH ___ ___ ___ ___ ___ STORM (think of the antonym of *over*)

🌀 YOUR TURN TO WRITE

> **TIP FOR TOP WRITERS!**
> When explaining how things happen, first **research** your subject. Then:
> - **start** with the cause;
> - **explain** the consequences (results);
> - **arrange** consequences in order of happening or of importance.

① Sometimes we need to do some research before we write an explanation to make sure we have our facts right.

  a. Choose one of these subjects: floods   fires   electricity blackouts

  b. Find out all you can about the subject by researching in books and encyclopedias. If available, you can also use the Internet.

② **Write** an **introduction** that defines and explains your topic and how it develops.

_____

_____

_____

_____

③ **Write** a **list** of what happens in sequence.

  1. _____

  2. _____

  3. _____

  4. _____

  5. _____

  6. _____

④ **Write a conclusion** to what happens in your event by writing about its **long-term** effects.

  Example: It can take up to 30 years to rebuild a city destroyed by an **earthquake**. Houses, shops, and factories have to be rebuilt. Roads and bridges must be built. Water and power supplies must be restored and sewage systems rebuilt.

_____

_____

_____

⑤ Using your answers to all of the questions so far, **write an explanation** of what happens in your event on your own paper.

Pros and cons are points **for and against** an idea that is being discussed. They are usually written in single sentences in order of importance, followed by a conclusion.

STRUCTURE

LANGUAGE

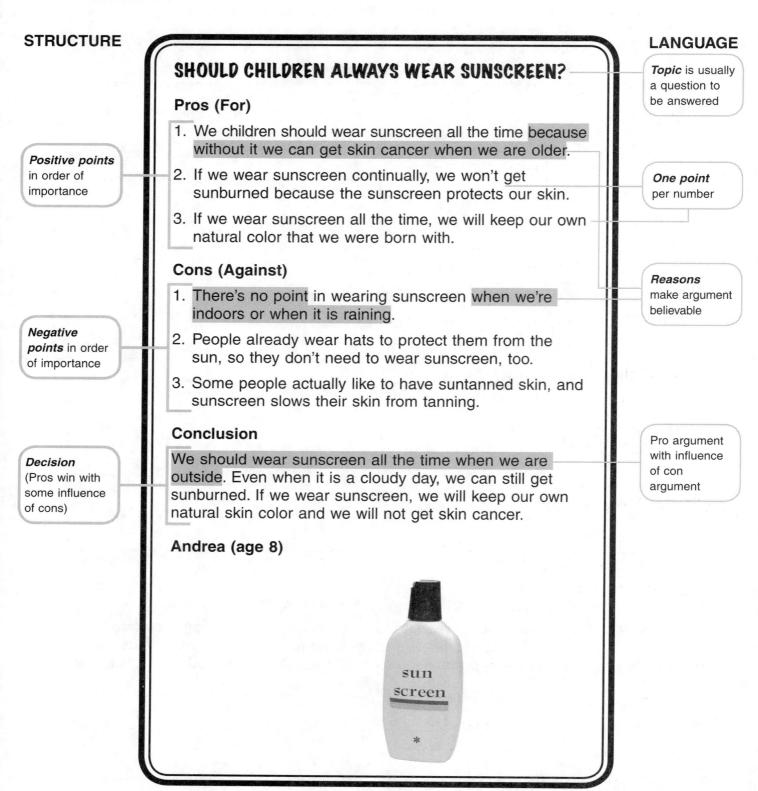

SHOULD CHILDREN ALWAYS WEAR SUNSCREEN?

Topic is usually a question to be answered

Pros (For)

Positive points in order of importance

1. We children should wear sunscreen all the time because without it we can get skin cancer when we are older.

2. If we wear sunscreen continually, we won't get sunburned because the sunscreen protects our skin.

One point per number

3. If we wear sunscreen all the time, we will keep our own natural color that we were born with.

Cons (Against)

Reasons make argument believable

1. There's no point in wearing sunscreen when we're indoors or when it is raining.

Negative points in order of importance

2. People already wear hats to protect them from the sun, so they don't need to wear sunscreen, too.

3. Some people actually like to have suntanned skin, and sunscreen slows their skin from tanning.

Conclusion

Decision (Pros win with some influence of cons)

We should wear sunscreen all the time when we are outside. Even when it is a cloudy day, we can still get sunburned. If we wear sunscreen, we will keep our own natural skin color and we will not get skin cancer.

Pro argument with influence of con argument

Andrea (age 8)

sun screen
*

✺ WHAT DID YOU READ?

①　**Circle** the correct answer. This discussion is about . . .

　　a. skin color　　　　　**b.** sunburn　　　　　**c.** wearing sunscreen

②　**Complete** this sentence. The most serious effect of going without sunscreen protection is . . .

_____

③　**Circle** the correct answer. When the writer refers to **natural color**, she is referring to . . .

　　a. skin color　　　　　**b.** clothing color　　　　　**c.** favorite color

④　The writer says sunscreen protects us from sunburn. Do you know what sunburn is? **Explain** in one **complete sentence**.

_____

_____

⑤　"There is no point in wearing sunscreen when we're indoors." Do you think this is a sensible point to make or a silly point? Why?

_____

⑥　**Circle** the correct answer. Hats protect us against sunburn by . . .

　　a. keeping our heads cool

　　b. keeping the sun's rays from our face and ears

　　c. keeping rain off our hair

⑦　The con case influenced the conclusion of this discussion. **What words** in the **first** sentence of the conclusion tell us this?

_____

✺ HOW IS IT WRITTEN?

①　**Circle** the correct word.

　　The first pro and the first con points are the **strongest / weakest** arguments of each case.

②　**Complete** this sentence.

　　Pro points are always　F ___ ___　the idea being discussed, and con points are always

　　A ___ ___ ___ ___ ___ ___ that idea.

③　**Complete** this sentence. Points are always listed in order from

　　S ___ ___ ___ ___ ___ EST to W ___ ___ ___ EST.

④　**Circle** the correct answer. Each point on this text is written as . . .

　　a. one sentence　　　**b.** one phrase　　　**c.** one paragraph

⑤　**Circle** the correct answer.

　　The conclusion **can / cannot** be influenced by the arguments of the losing case.

☼ SPELLING AND MEANING

Word Box	sunscreen	likely	wear	discussion
	cancer	continually	protect	argument
	sunburn	coloring	protection	conclusion

Sometimes letters represent more than one sound (e.g., the letter *c*).

C can be a hard sound as in *cat* or a soft sound as in *nice*. These can be tricky and need careful practice.

① **a. Write** three words from the word box that contain a **hard *c*.**

_____   _____   _____

b. The word *cancer* contains a hard *c* and a soft *c*. **Underline** the *soft c*. CANCER

② The letter *c* is usually a **soft *c*** if it is followed by the letter *e* (e.g. lettu**ce**, re**ce**ive). **Write** HARD or SOFT to describe the sound made by *c* in each of these words.

a. cell _____   **b.** cellophane _____

c. cake _____   **d.** recipe _____

e. decent _____   **f.** decay _____

③ **Insert** a word from the word box to complete each sentence.

a. People who work outdoors are more _____ to be sunburned than people who work indoors.

b. Raincoats and boots _____ us from the rain.

c. It rained _____ overnight, so the picnic was cancelled.

d. It is sensible to _____ hats in summertime.

e. Without sunscreen, people are at a higher risk of getting skin _____.

④ **Label** these pictures with a word from the word box.

a. _____   **b.** _____   **c.** _____

☼ GRAMMAR

Verbs do very important things in sentences. They tell us what **is** and what **happens**. They can also tell us **when** it is and **when** it happens.

We call this time-telling **tense**. If we want to change the time (tense) of a sentence we change the form of the verb.

> *Examples:* Josie **wears** sunscreen. (present tense)
>
> Josie **wore** sunscreen. (past tense)
>
> Josie **will wear** sunscreen. (future tense)

When we write **information reports** we write in the **present tense**, and when we write the **pros** and **cons** of a **discussion** we write them in the **present tense**, too.

① These sentences are all written in different tenses. **Name** the tenses.

  a. Yuki swims every day wearing sunscreen. _____ tense

  b. This summer will be very hot. _____ tense

  c. The sun burned the tips of my cat's ears. _____ tense

  d. Jack builds sand castles at the beach. _____ tense

② These sentences are all written in the present tense. **Rewrite** them in the **past** tense by changing their verbs.

  a. Maria always wears a T-shirt over her bathing suit in the pool.

  _____

  _____

  b. We pitch a tent for shade when we go on a picnic.

  _____

  _____

  c. The day is hot and bright, so we wear hats and sunscreen.

  _____

  _____

☼ PUNCTUATION—POSSESSIVE APOSTROPHE REVISION

Can you **help** the artist label the pictures and put his apostrophes in the right places?

a. the bees hive   **b.** the yachts sails   **c.** the birds nests

✺ FUN WITH WORDS

① Can you **match** these sounds to the things that make them?

a. rubber beach toy	
b. someone taking a picture	
c. waves	
d. someone eating chips	

click
squeak
crunch
splash

② I **rhyme** with *sister* and *mister*, and I am a sign of bad sunburn.

I am a ___ ___ ___ ___ ___ ___ ___.

③ It is a hot, sticky day. Mr. Tubb is hot and sticky, too. Can you **unscramble** the hot, sticky words for the air around him and the hot, sticky word that describes how his skin feels?

HUDIM _____ air

GGYUM _____ air

YEAMST _____ air

MMCLAY _____ skin

④ To protect yourself from sunburn at the beach, you will find all of these to be useful. **What** are they? You can guess from the rhyming clues.

a. I'm a happy rainbow **fella**: U ___ ___ ___ ___ LL ___

b. In a tube I have **been**: S ___ ___ ___ ___ ___ ___ ___ N

c. I'm a bowler and a beret and a bonnet, but I'm not a **bat**: ___ ___ ___

d. T-shirts do not **believe** in me: LONG SL ___ ___ ___ E

✺ YOUR TURN TO WRITE

TIP FOR TOP WRITERS!
When writing pros and cons for a discussion . . .
- **write** them in order of importance
- **write** in single sentences
- **try** to have an equal number of points for both sides
- **try** to answer the points on one side with points on the other

⊚ YOUR TURN TO WRITE (cont.)

① **Choose** one of these topics for discussion and **write** three points **for** it and three points **against** it. If you would like to choose a different topic, first get permission from your teacher.

- Every child should walk to school.
- All boys should play football.
- Everyone should learn to ride a bicycle.
- Students should not watch television during the week.
- Winter school holidays should be longer and summer holidays shorter.

Pros

1. _____

   _____

2. _____

   _____

3. _____

   _____

Cons

1. _____

   _____

2. _____

   _____

3. _____

   _____

② Now **write** a **conclusion** to your discussion after deciding which points make the strongest case, the pros or the cons. **Write** your final copy on a separate sheet of paper.

_____

_____

_____

_____

_____

_____

A **procedural recount** tells how a procedure (an activity or a process) was carried out in the sequence (order) that it was carried out.

STRUCTURE

LANGUAGE

HOW WE WATCHED ROOTS GROW

Introduction
(idea and plan)

Mrs. Russo told us how plants grow from seeds. Tom wished he could see how their roots grow under the ground, so Mrs. Russo said we could do an experiment to see them growing. She said we could make a plant viewer.

Procedure steps
in sequence

Time words
make sequence clear

Step 1: the container

She cut the top off a big plastic milk bottle. Then she cut one side off the box-shaped bit at an angle so that part of the bottom got cut off, too. This left three sides on a small base.

Step 2: the clear side

Michael found a clear plastic cooking oil bottle. Susie cut a rectangular piece out of it to use as a clear side for our plant viewer. Then she held the clear piece against the milk-bottle box so Mrs. Russo could stick it on with green tape.

Shape
adjective

Now our viewer had a see-through side. We filled it up with soil and Renee made it damp with a water sprayer. Then Tom and Len planted four bean seeds in the soil, close to the clear side of the viewer.

Because roots grow in darkness, Mrs. Russo found some black paper, and we cut out a rectangle to hang down in front of the clear side, like a curtain. She taped it across the top so it wouldn't fall off. We put a rubber band around the viewer and the curtain to make sure all light was kept out. Then we put the plant viewer in the cupboard for a week.

Comparison
to make use clear

Step 5: put on window sill and water

A week later the bean seeds had sprouted tiny leaves. Because leaves need sunlight to grow green, we put the viewer on the window sill. After that, we watered the plants every morning with the sprayer.

Factual adjectives

Every other day, we lifted the black paper curtain. Through the clear side we could see the bean roots. They were growing straight down the clear side of the viewer as fast as the leaves and the stem grew upwards. The roots were long and thin and white.

Facts only:
no imagination

Conclusion

Tom was very proud of what we had done. He gave a talk about our experiment at our school assembly.

WHAT DID YOU READ?

① **Circle** the correct answer. The main task of this text is to recount . . .

   a. roots   **b.** watering plants   **c.** an experiment about seeing roots grow

② **Circle** the correct answer. Tom . . .

   a. told us how plants grow from seeds

   b. wished he could see plant roots growing

   c. said the class could carry out an experiment

③ **Circle two** correct answers. The plant viewing box was made out of a . . .

   a. plastic milk bottle

   b. clear, plastic soft-drink bottle

   c. clear, plastic cooking oil bottle

④ **Why** did the plant viewer have one clear side?

   _____

⑤ **Complete** this sentence.

   Mrs. Russo used the green sticky tape to attach the _____ to the viewer

   and to stick the _____ to the top edge of the viewing side.

⑥ **Circle two** correct answers. When the experiment was finished, Tom discovered that . . .

   a. roots grow straight down   **b.** bean roots are green

   c. bean roots are thin   **d.** roots grow more slowly than leaves and stems

HOW IS IT WRITTEN?

① **Circle** the correct answer. The subject, an experiment to see plant roots grow, first appears in **paragraph 1 / paragraph 2**.

② The author uses many time words and phrases to show the order in which things were done. **Write** two time words that you find in paragraph 6.

   _____   _____

③ **Circle** the correct answer. This procedural recount contains . . .

   a. facts and opinions   **b.** facts only   **c.** instructions only

④ **Circle** the correct answer. This procedural recount tells how the class made a plant viewer . . .

   a. that didn't work   **b.** out of cardboard   **c.** in the order that they made it

⑤ **Circle** the correct answer. Which occurs in both the first and the last paragraphs to complete the recount?

   a. Mrs. Russo   **b.** the experiment   **c.** the idea of seeing how roots grow

✸ SPELLING AND MEANING

Word Box	experiment	through	straight	tape
	view	cupboard	upwards	taped
	piece	leaves	plastic	tapped

When a word ends with *–e*, then the vowel that comes before it is usually **long** (e.g., t**a**pe). We call this **bossy e** because it tells other vowels what to do. If there is no **bossy e** at the end, then the last vowel is usually **short** (e.g., t**a**p).

① **Name** the object in each picture and write SHORT or LONG underneath to describe the vowel sound.

a. R_____   **b.** T_____   **c.** M_____   **d.** T_____

_____   _____   _____   _____

② When we add *–ed* to a **short** vowelled verb, we **double** the last consonant (e.g., tap → ta**pp**ed). **Add *–ed*** to each of the following.

a. rap _____   **b.** drip _____

c. map _____   **d.** sip _____

③ The word ***cupboard*** contains a silent *p*. We don't pronounce it. **Circle** the silent letter in each of these words.

a. knife   **b.** numb   **c.** pneumonia   **d.** receipt

Some letters occur in groups (e.g., the letters *ie* when they make the sound *ee*). Always remember:

I* comes before *E (e.g., believe, piece) **except after *C*** (e.g., receive) or in words like *neighbor* and *weigh*.

④ **Insert *ie* correctly four times and *ei* correctly once** in the following:

a. He sighed with REL ___ ___ F.

b. Kelly is Mr. Ando's N ___ ___ CE.

c. May I have a P ___ ___ CE of that cake?

d. This is my REC ___ ___ PT for that book.

e. The city was under S ___ ___ GE by its enemies.

⊚ SPELLING AND MEANING (cont.)

⑤   **Write** a word from the word box on page 58 to explain these pictures.

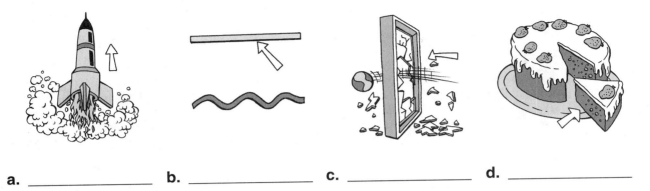

a. _____   b. _____   c. _____   d. _____

⊚ GRAMMAR

Adverbs of time (time words) are very important when you are writing a procedural recount. They help the reader understand exactly when things were done.

Example: We will go to a movie and eat something ***later***.

①   These are common adverbs of time. **Insert** them correctly in the following sentences.

then	first	afterwards	finally	early	beforehand

a. When you plant a tree, you must _____ dig a hole.

b. The sky turns red and gold _____ in the evening.

c. He planted, watered, and fertilized his cornfield, and _____, in the summer he harvested it.

d. The scientist conducted an experiment, _____ he wrote a report on it.

e. Be sure to pack your vacation gear _____ .

f. The storm raged and the ground was littered with hailstones _____ .

②   **Underline** all the **adverbs of time** you find in these sentences.

   a. Peter and Luke later regretted their decision to steal.

   b. In the experiments to grow crystals, we always had to handle the chemicals carefully.

   c. We never learned about ballet in our dance class.

   d. Please water the plants now because they really need it.

   e. Tonight it will be possible to see a full moon.

✺ GRAMMAR (cont.)

③ Look at these two pictures. **Write** a sentence using the adverb *after* to explain what is happening in them.

_____

_____

✺ PUNCTUATION—REVISION

① **Insert** all missing apostrophes in these contractions.

a. Im going, youre going, hes going. In fact, were all going to the Science Expo in the city.

b. Wheres the sticky tape to wrap this package?

c. Theyve all gone to the aquarium to study fish.

d. It isnt true that it can rain cats and dogs.

e. Weve been collecting money to buy seeds for a class garden.

② **Circle** all the letters that should be capitalized.

a. new zealand and norway are both famous for their glaciers.

b. the kalahari, sahara, gobi, and atacama are all barren deserts.

c. the russian yuri gagarin, in his spacecraft *vostok I*, was the first man in space.

d. astronomers can tell us all about planets like mars, jupiter, and saturn.

e. the pacific ocean has a powerful influence on the weather of hawaii.

✺ FUN WITH WORDS

① Scientists do lots of experiments to find out how and why things work. The people below are all scientists. Can you **complete** their names?

a. G __ __ LOGIST   I study rocks.

b. M __ __ __ __ LURGIST   I study metals.

c. CH __ __ IST   I study chemicals.

d. ENT __ M __ L __ GIST   I study insects.

e. B __ T __ __IST   I study plants.

FUN WITH WORDS (cont.)

② We are also scientists. Can you **match** us to our fields of study?

a. astronomer		oceans and their currents	
b. marine biologist		volcanoes	
c. oceanographer		creatures of the sea	
d. climatologist		moon and the stars	
e. vulcanologist		weather patterns of the world	

The clear side of the plant viewer in the text at the beginning of this lesson was described as **see-through**. It could also have been called a **transparent** side.

The prefix **trans–** means **through** or **across**. This side could be seen through.

③ Do you **know** these **trans–** words?

    a. TRANSP __ R __ __ T (e.g., window glass)

    b. TRANS __ C __ __ NIC (e.g., across the ocean)

    c. TRANS __ __ T (e.g., to send a radio or television signal)

    d. TRANSN __ T __ __ N __ L (e.g., a company with branches in many countries)

④ Can you **complete** this scientific explanation?

When light shines through a raindrop or a diamond, it creates a rainbow-colored light. Raindrops and diamonds are TRANS __ __ __ __ __ T. They let light shine through them and break it up into its colors.

⑤ These are the colors of a rainbow. Can you unscramble them?

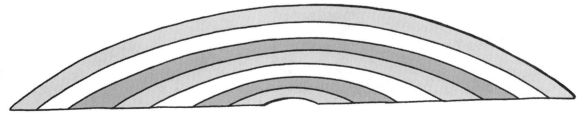

    a. DER: _____

    b. GEROAN: _____

    c. LLOWYE: _____

    d. NEEGR: _____

    e. LUEB: _____

    f. DIGOIN: _____

    g. TELIOV: _____

JOKE

Q: What two things can you never eat for breakfast?
A: Lunch and dinner.

YOUR TURN TO WRITE

TIP FOR TOP WRITERS!

When writing a procedural recount:
1. **Stick** to the facts.
2. **Connect** the facts with time words.
3. **Put** the facts in order.
4. **Link** your last paragraph to your first.

---

① Professor Schmidt is conducting an experiment. Can you **complete** his explanation of what his experiment proves?

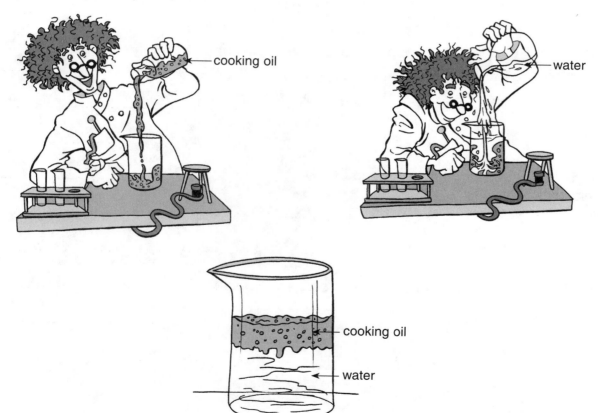

I, Professor Hans Schmidt, have demonstrated that _____ weighs less than

_____ because, even though I poured it into the glass _____, it is now

floating on top of the water.

YOUR TURN TO WRITE (cont.)

② Think about everything Professor Schmidt did to conduct his experiment—the equipment he had to gather, the materials he used, the details of the experiment itself, and the order in which he conducted it. Then write a procedural recount of his experiment on the following lines.

Introduction (What did the professor want to find out?) _____

_____

_____

_____

Paragraph 2 (Gathering equipment and materials) _____

_____

_____

_____

Paragraph 3 (What the professor did first) _____

_____

_____

_____

Paragraph 4 (What he did next) _____

_____

_____

_____

Conclusion (What the experiment proved) _____

_____

_____

_____

③ Using your own paper, outline a procedural recount of the topic of your choice. Then rewrite your final copy after you have checked for spelling and punctuation.

When we write a **response** to a picture, we **explain** what we see and what we **think** and **feel** about what we see.

STRUCTURE   **LANGUAGE**

Introduction

This photo was taken in Sideshow Alley at a country fair. It is a picture of one of the rides. We can see two boys driving a car on the end of one of the arms of a machine.

Clear, short sentences

Body of response

The arms of the machine are raised. The middle section must be an engine that makes the arms go around and around. It is covered with flashing lights and looks exciting.

Fact

Opinion

Details and response

The ticket booth is advertising a special deal of four dollars a ride or four rides for ten dollars. If you pay ten dollars, you can ride on the Cup and Saucer, this car ride, the Big Bubble, and the motorbikes. The boys probably wouldn't want to ride in a cup and saucer, so I think they only paid for one ride.

Fact

Opinion

Details and response

The little cars have headlights like great big eyes, and the ticket booth is painted with happy pictures. Even though this is not a color photo, I can imagine all the little cars painted in bright colors. All the colored lights would be flashing red and green and yellow. I am sure there is loud, happy music playing as the cars go around. No wonder the boy on the left is smiling.

Comparison to make picture clear

Writer's impression or feeling

Direction to help reader

Details and response

The boy on the right is looking back over his shoulder. Perhaps he is looking at his parents watching him drive. He has the steering wheel so I think he feels very proud of himself.

Writer's own opinion

Conclusion a personal decision

I would really like to go to a fair like this one day.

✺ WHAT DID YOU READ?

① **Circle** the correct answer. Sideshow Alley is . . .

    a. a movie theater

    b. a street of rides and games at a fair

    c. another name for a country fair

② How much did each boy pay for his one ride? _____

③ **Name** two other rides the boys could have chosen.

_____   _____

④ The writer thinks one boy is feeling very proud.

    a. Do you **agree**? _____

    b. Can you **explain** why he might feel proud? _____

⑤ **Circle all** the correct answers. Looking at this picture makes the writer . . .

    a. use imagination   **b.** feel sad

    c. feel happy   **d.** want to go to a fair

✺ HOW IS IT WRITTEN?

① **Circle** the correct answer: **True** or **False**

    The first paragraph tells us what is happening in the picture and where it is happening.

② **Complete** this sentence.

    This response includes both F ___ ___ TS and OP ___ N ___ ONS.

③ **Read** paragraph 2 carefully and then **circle** the **two** correct answers.

    The opinion sentences in this paragraph are . . .

    a. the first sentence   **b.** the second sentence   **c.** the third sentence

④ Direction words help the reader see which part of the picture you are describing. **Write** one direction you find in the text.

_____

⑤ **Insert** these verbs in the following sentences to correctly complete the paragraph.

thinks   imagines   describes

The writer _____ what he sees. He puts himself in the place of the boys

in the picture and _____ what they must be feeling. He uses his senses to tell

us what he _____ the colors and the sounds of a fair might be.

✺ SPELLING AND MEANING

Word Box	background	whether	electricity	machine
	foreground	weather	power	booth
	alley	different	center	ticket

When learning the words in the word box, don't be put off by their size. **Break** them into **smaller words** (e.g., back-ground) or into **syllables** (e.g., e-lec-tri-ci-ty).

Remember, every big word is only a group of smaller words or syllables.

① **Complete** these sentences with a word from the word box.

   a. The truck is in the _____ of the picture.

   b. The car is in the _____ of the picture.

② **Insert** a word from the word box in these sentences.

   a. John couldn't decide _____ to go to the movies or the beach.

   b. If the _____ is good, the fair will be a success.

   c. Fred strolled down the narrow, winding _____.

   d. Lightning is natural _____ in the air.

   e. Your prize is _____ from mine. Mine is a medal, but yours is a star.

③ **Which word** from the word box would describe the position of all the arrowed items in these pictures? _____

✿ SPELLING AND MEANING (cont.)

④ *Fore* means **in front**. Can you **complete** these *fore* words?

a. FORE ___ ___ ___ ___ (part of your face)

b. FORE ___ ___ ___ (wrist to elbow)

c. ___ ___ FORE (opposite of "after")

d. FORE ___ ___ ___ ___ ___ ___ (lower front of picture)

e. FORE ___ ___ ___ (person in charge of a construction team)

⑤ **Circle** the correct answer.

Power and *electricity* can mean the **same** thing. They are **synonyms / antonyms**.

✿ GRAMMAR

Plural subjects (more than one) are always followed by the **plural form of the verb**.
Single subjects are followed by the **singular form of the verb**.

Examples: The <u>crane</u> (singular) <u>is lifting</u> (singular) that car.

The <u>cranes</u> (plural) <u>are lifting</u> (plural) that car.

① **Circle** the correct answer in these sentences.

a. Chloe and Yusuf **is / are** going to the show.

b. Little children **is / are** enjoying the cup and saucer ride.

c. My dad **is / are** playing the Ring Toss game.

d. All of the boys **is / are** driving bumper cars.

When we use a **group noun** to name **one** gathering of people, animals, or things, we usually use the **singular form of the verb**. This is because a group noun names **one** group.

Examples: The <u>audience</u> (group noun) <u>was</u> (singular verb) silent during the concert.

The <u>fleet</u> (group noun) <u>is sailing</u> (singular verb) south.

② **Circle** the correct answer in these sentences.

a. A crowd of spectators **was / were** watching the Grand Parade.

b. A pair of pigeons **is / are** asleep in the rafters.

c. A herd of cattle **is / are** to be exhibited in the main arena.

d. A clutch of chickens **is / are** on display in the poultry shed.

③ **Read** these sentences carefully and then **circle** the correct answers.

a. Claudia and Aldo **is / are** playing a piano duet.

b. That swarm of bees **is / are** nesting in the roof of the ticket booth.

c. Mrs. Leonello **make / makes** delicious cotton candy.

d. A team of horses **is / are** pulling a wagon of hay.

e. Twelve boys **is / are** lined up to buy bumper car rides.

☼ PUNCTUATION—REVISION

Insert all the missing capitalization and punctuation. (Think about capital letters, commas, and periods.)

one of the great fairs of the world is the calgary stampede in canada. it is an exhibition of cattle horses and horse-riding skills. every year people come from as far afield as argentina australia new zealand the united states and even mongolia to compete in the calgary stampede. they pit their skills against each other in competitions like rounding up roping cattle and riding bulls. in addition to the cattle and horse events there are all the usual fair activities including displays of local produce exhibitions of local craftwork and all the games and rides of sideshow alley

☼ FUN WITH WORDS

① Fairs usually include a display of produce—grains, fruits, and vegetables grown locally. **Sort** these produce items into the right wheelbarrows.

wheat	bananas	potatoes	barley	grapes	strawberries	carrots	millet
pineapples	rye	pumpkin	squash	lettuce	cabbage	rice	lemons
beans	mangoes	corn	pears				

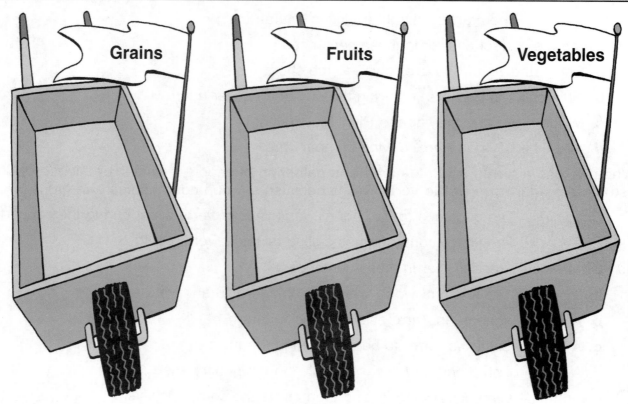

Grains **Fruits** **Vegetables**

② These are all berries. Use the clues beside them to fill in the missing letters.

a. B ___ ___ ___ ___ BERRY (I rhyme with *tack*.)

b. B ___ ___ ___ BERRY (I am the color of very cold hands.)

c. S ___ ___ ___ ___ BERRY (I am what's left after wheat is harvested.)

d. R ___ ___ ___ BERRY (I am red and a popular flavor for iced tea.)

e. B ___ ___ ___ ___ ___ BERRY (I sound like part of "boys 'n girls.")

☼ FUN WITH WORDS (cont.)

③ County fairs also feature the judging of farm animals. Can you unscramble these animals listed for judging?

a. SPIG _____   **b.** PEESH _____   **c.** TTCAEL _____

d. TOAGS _____   **e.** CHKNSIEC _____   **f.** SHSOER _____

④ I'm a new animal at some county fairs. My homeland is South America.

I am an A___P___CA.

⑤ To win at this game, you must throw the balls into the clown's mouth and choose which lanes you want them to land in. Choose the correct lanes by letter and you will be a winner!

I O Z C H M Q P A N E D

GRAND C __ __ __ __ __ __ N

⑥ You will find us at a fair. What are we?

a. A vertical turning wheel of chairs: I am a F __ __ __ __ S W __ __ __ L.

b. A sticky, pink, fluffy sweet: I am C __ __ __ __ __ C __ __ __ __.

c. Little cars that bump into each other: We are B __ __ __ __ R C __ __ __ __.

d. Displays of fruits and vegetables: We are PR __ __ __ __ E.

☼ YOUR TURN TO WRITE

> **TIP FOR TOP WRITERS!**
> When writing a response to a picture:
> • **Write** the place (and the time, if you can).
> • **Write** what is happening (facts).
> • **Write** what you think (opinion).
> • **Write** any conclusion (wish, decision) you reach.

☀ YOUR TURN TO WRITE (cont.)

① Look closely at this picture.

a. Make a **list** of **facts** (what you see in the picture).

_____   _____

_____   _____

_____   _____

_____   _____

b. Make a **list** of your **thoughts** about the picture (e.g., Would you like to be there? Are the people happy?).

_____   _____

_____   _____

_____   _____

c. Write a **where/when** introduction to your response.

_____

_____

_____

_____

d. Write a **conclusion** to your response, saying whether you would or would not like to do what the people in the picture are doing. Explain why you think that.

_____

_____

_____

② Using all of your answers above, **write** a **response** to this picture on your own paper.

When we write a **biography**, we are recounting the **life** and **achievements** of someone. A **time line** records the same information in a **visual** way.

STRUCTURE

LANGUAGE

THE BIOGRAPHY

Shirley Smith (Mum Shirl)

Introduction name, date, and place of birth

Shirley Smith was an Aborigine of the Wiradjuri people of New South Wales, Australia. She was born in Cowra in 1924 and lived there until her family moved to Sydney when she was a young woman.

In the late 1930s, she began to visit people in jail because she knew they were lonely and had no one to talk to. She kept visiting them when they came home from jail and helped them find work and places to live. She became known as Mum Shirl by all the people she helped.

Achievements in the order that they happened

At the same time, Mum Shirl began to take children who were unhappy or homeless or whose parents were sick into her own home. Over her lifetime, she was mother to over 60 children.

Because she saw the need for better services, she was one of the people who set up the Aboriginal Medical and Legal Services in 1971 and 1972. Her work for other people was tireless.

Conclusion date of death; personal statement about person

In 1985, Mum Shirl was awarded an Order of Australia in recognition of her lifetime's work on behalf of people in need. When she died in 1998, thousands of people from all walks of life felt that they had lost a friend. They felt that they had been privileged to know a truly good person.

Mostly facts used in research projects

Time words make sequence clear

Good choice of adjective

Specific award granted

THE TIME LINE

Life of Mum Shirl

Earliest years on the left to later years on the right

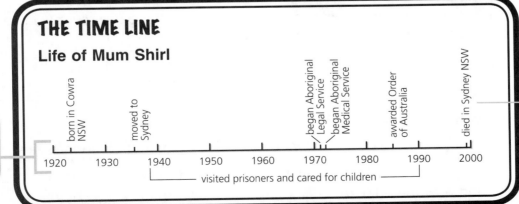

Only a few necessary words for each important date

☼ BIOGRAPHY OR TIME LINE? WHAT ARE THE DIFFERENCES?

① **Complete** this sentence.

A biography is written in S ___ NT ___ ___ ___ ES and a time line is written in

short PH ___ ___ ___ ES.

② **Circle all** the correct answers. In a biography, key points are . . .

a. dates of birth and death   **b.** color of shoes

c. places of birth and death   **d.** dates of important events in life

e. family and friends   **f.** favorite song

g. opinions of others   **h.** personality

③ **Circle** the correct answer: **True / False**

Both a biography and a time line are arranged in chronological order (order of events).

④ **Circle** the correct answer.

The time line and the biography **do / do not** contain exactly the same information.

⑤ Which writing allows you to say what other people think about your person: the biography or the time line? _____

⑥ Sometimes it is not possible to find out exactly when something happened in your person's life. In this case, would you write a biography or a time line?

_____

⑦ If you were writing about an inventor who invented something new every single year, would it be more sensible to write a biography or a time line? Why?

_____

_____

⑧ **Complete** the following sentences.

a. A _____ allows us to see the span of someone's life at a glance.

b. A _____ lets us find out what someone did during his or her life and why and how they did so.

☼ YOUR TURN TO WRITE

> **TIP FOR TOP WRITERS!**
> When you write a biography . . .
> - **Use** your own words (do **not** copy straight from a book or the Internet).
> - **Include** important dates and places.
> - **Write** events in the order that they occurred in your person's life.
> - **Explain** why your person is important.

① **Outline** a short biography below of someone in your family, starting with his or her birth and ending with who he or she is and what he or she is doing now. Then **write** your final biography on your own paper.

Date and place of birth _____

_____

Main events in life _____

_____

_____

_____

_____

_____

_____

How you feel about this person _____

_____

_____

② **Complete** a time line of your own life starting with your birth. Use the time line below as a guide and mark on it the dates that are special in your life. Then above those dates, write what happened at that time to make the date special. Each space represents one year. The first will be the year you were born. **Rewrite** your final time line on your own paper.

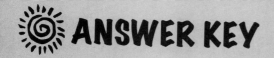

LESSON 1   PAGES 6-11

What did you read?
① False
② b
③ c
④ a
⑤ d
⑥ The end of a glacier is tall and flat-faced like a wall. It is all blue-green ice.
⑦ The brown streaks are made by the earth the glacier traveled through and picked up.

How is it written?
① yesterday, first, today, tomorrow
② crossed, drove, stopped, looked, stayed, bought
③ black-and-white pictures
④ they are green-brown/they are vicious/they rip up soft parts of cars/they deflate tires

Spelling and meaning
① a. bought
   b. peek
   c. diary
   d. tires
   e. peak
   f. dairy
② a. N
   b. N
   c. N
   d. Y
③ herd, fern; whirl, bird; fur, furl; heard, pearl
④ a. pearl
   b. heard
   c. furl

Grammar
① a. Glaciers (are) rivers of ice.
   b. Harry (climbed) the glacier wall.
   c. A glacier climber (carries) rope, spikes, and a small hammer.
② a. The waters of mountain lakes are very cold.
   b. Snowboarding and skiing are popular sports in the Alps.
   c. Mountain air is very thin.
③ a. Glaciers carry stones in their ice, but rivers carry silt in their waters.
   b. Glaciers begin in alpine lakes, but rivers begin in mountain rains.
   c. Thin ice looks white, but thick ice looks blue or green.

Punctuation
Some mountains are famous for their snow—mountains like Everest in Nepal, Fuji in Japan, the Matterhorn in Austria, and Tongariro in New Zealand. Other mountains, like Mt. St. Helens in the United States, Vesuvius in Italy, Pinatubo in the Philippines, and Gunung Agung in Indonesia, are volcanic and famous for boiling lava and explosions.

Fun with words
① mild, cool, chilly, cold, icy
② a. cool
   b. icy
   c. cold
③ a. glacier
   b. lake
   c. billabong
   d. tide
④ a. skis
   b. sled
   c. toboggan
   d. chair lift
⑤ mountain goat

Your turn to write
① Possible answer:
   1. wake
   2. wash
   3. dress
   4. eat
   5. brush teeth
② 1. dog chased my cat
   2. cat raced up tree
   3. cat wouldn't come down
   4. I climbed tree
   5. cat climbed higher
   6. I climbed higher
   7. both too frightened to climb down

LESSON 2   PAGES 12-19

What did you read?
① False
② the 19th Battalion of Chocolate Wheatens
③ a. Wheaten   b. Tim Tam
④ defeats
⑤ c
⑥ a
⑦ b

How is it written?
① a
② sequence
③ headquarters, regiment, battalion, division, siege
④ a, c
⑤ a

Spelling and meaning
① a. cook/ie
   b. ic/ing
   c. fal/ter
   d. dec/la/ra/tion
   e. de/ci/sive
   f. use/less
② a. armor, capital, icing
   b. dangerous, defeat, division

c. 1. bow 2. cookie 3. shield 4. top
d. siege, sign, single
e. decisive, declaration, falter, useless, weapon
③ a. humor
   b. clamor
   c. vigor

Grammar

① a. abstract
   b. group
   c. group
   d. group, abstract, group
② a. clutch
   b. pack
   c. fleet
   d. school
   e. congregation
③ a. generosity
   b. leadership
   c. mercy
   d. courtesy

Punctuation

a. Is India north or south of the equator?
b. Good heavens! That pink pig is flying!
c. Chile's flag is sky blue with a big yellow sun in the middle.
d. What is the national language of Brazil?

Fun with words

① a. pride
   b. pod
   c. bunch
   d. herd
   e. army
   f. team
③ a. admiral, captain, seaman
   b. principal, vice principal, teacher, student
   c. president, senator, governor, mayor

LESSON 3   PAGES 20-25

What did you read?

① c
② In the packet of grass seeds there must also have been weed seeds.
③ The cat ate him because he was too fat to run away.
④ in Ryde
⑤ a
⑥ apple cider
⑦ c
⑧ She was so thin she slipped down her straw into the lemonade.
⑨ birds

How is it written?

① subject
② a, b
③ Ryde, died, inside

Spelling and meaning

① a. flea
   b. flue
   c. pane
② sneak, spy, creep, tattle, rob
③ a. creep
   b. rob
   c. sneak
   d. watch
④ a. ferment
   b. either
   c. pain
   d. packet
   e. beard
⑤ a. wrench
   b. wring
   c. wrong
   d. write
   e. wriggle
⑥ a. white
   b. dry
   c. cloudy
   d. going
   e. full

Grammar

① a. tall, thin, red, baggy
   b. skinny, bandy, round, little, round, black
② a. lonely, jolly
   b. selfish, happy
   c. thoughtful, kind
③ a. visible, invisible, naked
   b. ripe, unripe
   c. venomous, green, harmless

Punctuation

① isn't, don't
② haven't, She's

Fun with words

① a. tickles
   b. funny
   c. head
   d. spinning
② a. gyring, gimbling
   b. wabe
   c. brillig
   d. slithy
⑤ a. clown
   b. magician
   c. ventriloquist

Your turn to write

① ramble
② a. Who couldn't remember her name
   b. Who sported an awful black shiner
   c. Who only ate water with bran

LESSON 4 PAGES 26-31

What did you read?
① action
② **a.** nectar and pollen-collecting
   b. making honey
③ False
④ She is too big.
⑤ Nurses
⑥ b
⑦ what it eats

How is it written?
① hives are not always dome-shaped/queen lives in bottom story/queen cannot enter other floors/ queen is bigger than other bees
② nectar/pollen/drone/sacs/nurse/queen
③ a, d
④ shape, color, size, number

Spelling and meaning
① **a.** collect
   b. Pollen
   c. communicate
   d. Entrance
   e. dome
② **a.** horses
   b. fish
   c. pigs
   d. cows
   e. geese
   f. koalas
③ **a.** creatures
   b. stories
   c. burrows
   d. hives
   e. hatcheries
   f. hutches
④ **a.** to cause to feel boredom
   b. male pig
   c. equipment used to control a horse
   d. relating to a wedding
   e. passenger boat
   f. tiny mythical creature with wings

Grammar
① **a.** hunt
   b. hibernate
   c. are
   d. is
   e. watch
② **a.** were sunning
   b. is resting
   c. were hunting
   d. was cruising
③ **b.** hibernate
   c. defend

Punctuation
a. Ants stand guard, hunt, trap, build, climb, and migrate.
b. Pandas are known for sleeping, eating, and sleeping again.
c. Dolphins are famed for diving, leaping out of the water, barrelling, and somersaulting.

Fun with words
① **a.** nestling
   b. calf
   c. cub
   d. fingerling
   e. calf
   f. cygnet
② owl, opossum, raccoon, bat, jaguar
③ **a.** eyrie
   b. warren
   c. mound
   d. lair

LESSON 5 PAGES 32-37

What did you read?
① c
② a, b
③ dust, cobwebs
④ It smelled like sunshine and grease and chopped wood all mixed together.
⑤ wait
⑥ to give him something to do on a rainy day

How is it written?
① b
② b, c
③ c
④ a, c
⑤ adjectives

Spelling and meaning
① **a.** straight
   b. weight
   c. label
   d. idle
   e. sneeze
② grease
③ **a.** wait
   b. peal
   c. reeds
   d. reel
   e. pail
   f. real
   g. peel
④ **a.** crooked
   b. cry
   c. busy
   d. demolish
   e. open

76

Grammar

① a. complex
   b. compound
   c. compound
   d. complex
② a. (Unless there is a breeze,) the paint won't dry.
   b. (While we were in the old shed,) we saw a redback spider.
   c. (Even though there were cobwebs in the attic,) we were not frightened.
③ Possible sentences:
   a. Unless it is raining, I will go to the bakery.
   b. Although it is so old, the school still has not fallen down.
   c. When you are here, we will paint the fence.

Punctuation

① a. "Does dust make you sneeze?" Ibrahim asked Paul.
   b. "Hand me some more nails," the carpenter told his apprentice.
② a. "Help!" he shouted. "The wind is lifting the roof off!"
   b. "I know you like the beach," said Melissa, "but I prefer the mountains."

Fun with words

① a. bottles   b. comics
   c. lamps   d. tools
② a. lighthouse   b. igloo
   c. mosque   d. observatory
③ a. hammer
   b. saw
   c. chisel
   d. wrench
   e. screwdriver
⑤ a. plum   b. bob → plumb bob

LESSON 6   PAGES 38–43

What did you read?

① fourth-graders
② a. bright colors
   b. loud music
③ a. laziness/bad attitudes
   b. swearing
④ False
⑤ d

How is it written?

① I believe
② b
③ b
④ *Bugs Bunny* and *Road Runner* show an average of 55 violent acts per hour.
⑤ Dr. Patricia Edgar, the International Coalition Against Violence
⑥ a, c, e

Spelling and meaning

① a. break into a conversation
   b. between countries
   c. between states
   d. point where two roads meet
   e. come between two quarrelling people
   f. get in the way of someone's work
② a. telescope
   b. television
   c. telephone
③ a. community
   b. influence
   c. negative
   d. extremely
   e. international

Grammar

① a. early
   b. eagerly
   c. usually, very
   d. cheaply
   e. positively
② a. today (when)
   b. usually (when)
   c. there (where)
   d. internationally (where)
   e. negatively (how)

Punctuation

I firmly believe that if you have a pet you should look after it as if it is a member of your family. After all, it lives in the same house as you and shares every part of your life, probably even more closely than your friends do.

So what does looking after your pet like a member of your family mean? First, it means your pet is fed daily. It means it is fed what is right for its breed, not just scraps from the kitchen. It means you make sure it has plenty of clean water to drink every day.

Like us, pets feel the heat and the cold. In winter you must make sure it has a warm, dry shelter out of the wind and rain, and in summer you must see that it has lots of cool shade to protect it from the heat.

If it is sick you take it to the vet, and if it is miserable you play with it and reassure it that it is your friend. We owe our pets the same loyal friendship they give us.

Fun with words

① a. story in cartoon format
   b. serious, acted story about people and events
   c. program discussing real events and issues
   d. how to improve your life, house, garden, etc.
   e. program designed to make you laugh
   f. competition with competitors and prizes

② 1. village, 2. town, 3. city, 4. metropolis
③ **a.** quite
   b. very
   c. extremely
④ **a.** a group of adults
   b. the president
   c. your football team
   d. a judge
   e. a minister named Smith

LESSON 7   PAGES 44-49

What did you read?
① b
② a
③ c
④ **a.** It clogs breathing.
   b. It stings the eyes.
⑤ It damages its parts.
⑥ The topsoil, which has nutrients for plants, has been blown away.

How is it written?
① True
② A dust storm is a moving wall of dust.
③ The dust storms that became known as the Dust Bowl affected five U.S. states.
④ largest, smallest
⑤ problem

Spelling and meaning
① **a.** traveling
   b. moving
   c. proving
   d. labeling
   e. deciding
② **a.** a long time without rain
   b. make
   c. occasionally
   d. without covering
③ **a.** invisible
   b. inaudible
   c. intangible
④ **a.** inaudible
   b. invisible
   c. intangible
⑤ **a.** write
   b. right
   c. bear
   d. bare

Grammar—Adverb Revision
① **a.** absolutely
   b. less
   c. very
② **a.** wildly
   b. tomorrow
   c. very

Punctuation
① **a.** farmer's
   b. plant's
   c. student's
   d. meteorologist's
② **a.** birds'
   b. horses'
   c. Farmers'

Fun with words
① **a.** arid
   b. barren
   c. dusty
   d. thirsty
② dry, dusty, cracked, hot, burning, bare, arid, empty, dead, thirsty, wilted, bony, dying, hungry, withered
③ **a.** camel
   b. oasis
   c. date
④ **a.** hurricane
   b. cyclone
   c. tornado
   d. gale
   e. typhoon
   f. thunderstorm

LESSON 8   PAGES 50-55

What did you read?
① c
② the higher risk of getting skin cancer
③ a
④ The UV rays of the sun burn the skin until it turns red and blisters.
⑤ A sensible point, because when we are inside, our entire bodies are protected from the sun, so we don't need any sunscreen.
⑥ b
⑦ all the time when we are outside

How is it written?
① strongest
② for, against
③ strongest, weakest
④ a
⑤ can

Spelling and meaning
① **a.** sunscreen, discussion, cancer, continually, coloring, protect, protection, conclusion
   b. cancer
② **a.** soft
   b. soft
   c. hard
   d. soft
   e. soft
   f. hard

③ a. likely
   b. protect
   c. continually
   d. wear
   e. cancer
④ a. discussion
   b. argument
   c. protection

Grammar
① a. present
   b. future
   c. past
   d. present
② a. Maria always **wore** a T-shirt over her bathing suit in the pool.
   b. We **pitched** a tent for shade when we **went** on a picnic.
   c. The day **was** hot and bright, so we **wore** hats and sunscreen.

Punctuation
a. bees'
b. yachts'
c. birds'

Fun with words
① a. squeak
   b. click
   c. splash
   d. crunch
② blister
③ **Air:** humid, muggy, steamy; **Skin:** clammy
④ a. umbrella
   b. sunscreen
   c. hat
   d. sleeve

LESSON 9   PAGES 56-63

What did you read?
① c
② b
③ a, c
④ to allow the students to see what was inside
⑤ clear side, curtain
⑥ a, c

How is it written?
① paragraph 1
② A week later/After that/every morning
③ b
④ c
⑤ b

Spelling and meaning
① a. rope (long)
   b. top (short)
   c. mop (short)
   d. tape (long)

② a. rapped   b. dripped
   c. mapped   d. sipped
③ a. **k**nife   b. num**b**
   c. **p**neumonia   d. receip**t**
④ a. relief   b. niece
   c. piece   d. receipt
   e. siege
⑤ a. upwards   b. straight
   c. through   d. piece

Grammar
① a. first
   b. early
   c. finally (or then)
   d. then
   e. beforehand
   f. afterwards
② a. later
   b. always
   c. never
   d. now
   e. Tonight
③ Possible answer: The boy went outside and looked at the moon through a telescope after he read about the moon in a book.

Punctuation—Revision
① a. I'm, you're, he's, we're
   b. Where's
   c. They've
   d. isn't
   e. We've
② a. **N**ew **Z**ealand and **N**orway are both famous for their glaciers.
   b. **T**he **K**alahari, **S**ahara, **G**obi, and **A**tacama are all barren deserts.
   c. **T**he **R**ussian **Y**uri **G**agarin, in his spacecraft *Vostok I*, was the first man in space.
   d. **A**stronomers can tell us about planets like **M**ars, **J**upiter, and **S**aturn.
   e. **T**he **P**acific **O**cean has a powerful influence on the weather of **H**awaii.

Fun with words
① a. geologist
   b. metallurgist
   c. chemist
   d. entomologist
   e. botanist
② a. moon and the stars
   b. creatures of the sea
   c. oceans and their currents
   d. weather patterns of the world
   e. volcanoes
③ a. transparent
   b. transoceanic
   c. transmit
   d. transnational

④ translucent
⑤ **a.** red
   b. orange
   c. yellow
   d. green
   e. blue
   f. indigo
   g. violet

Your turn to write
① I, Professor Hans Schmidt, have demonstrated that **oil** weighs less than **water** because, even though I poured it into the glass **first**, it is now floating on top of the water.

LESSON 10   PAGES 64-70

What did you read?
① b
② four dollars
③ Cup and Saucer/motorbikes/the Big Bubble
④ Possible answer: **a.** Yes
   b. because he is the driver of the car
⑤ a, c, d

How is it written?
① True
② facts, opinions
③ b, c
④ on the left, on the right
⑤ The writer **describes** what he sees. He puts himself in the place of the boys in the picture and **imagines** what they must be feeling. He uses his senses to tell us what he **thinks** the colors and the sounds of a fair might be.

Spelling and meaning
① **a.** background
   b. foreground
② **a.** whether
   b. weather
   c. alley
   d. electricity
   e. different
③ center
④ **a.** forehead
   b. forearm
   c. before
   d. foreground
   e. foreman
⑤ synonyms

Grammar
① **a.** are
   b. are
   c. is
   d. are
② **a.** was
   b. is
   c. is
   d. is

③ **a.** are
   b. is
   c. makes
   d. is
   e. are

Punctuation—Revision
One of the great fairs of the world is the Calgary Stampede in Canada. It is an exhibition of cattle, horses, and horse-riding skills. Every year people come from as far afield as Argentina, Australia, New Zealand, the United States, and even Mongolia to compete in the Calgary Stampede. They pit their skills against each other in competitions like rounding up, roping cattle, and riding bulls. In addition to the cattle and horse events, there are all the usual fair activities, including displays of local produce, exhibitions of local craftwork, and all the games and rides of Sideshow Alley.

Fun with words
① **Grain:** wheat, barley, millet, rye, rice
   Fruits: bananas, grapes, strawberries, pineapples, lemons, mangoes, pears
   Vegetables: potatoes, carrots, pumpkin, squash, lettuce, cabbage, beans, corn
② **a.** blackberry
   b. blueberry
   c. strawberry
   d. raspberry
   e. boysenberry
③ **a.** pigs
   b. sheep
   c. cattle
   d. goats
   e. chickens
   f. horses
④ alpaca
⑤ Grand Champion
⑥ **a.** ferris wheel
   b. cotton candy
   c. bumper cars
   d. produce

LESSON 11   PAGES 71-73

Biography or time line?
What are the differences?
① sentences, phrases
② a, c, d, e, g, h
③ True
④ do not
⑤ the biography
⑥ a biography
⑦ Possible answer: It would be sensible to write a biography because a time line would be too crowded. You would not mention every invention.
⑧ **a.** time line
   b. biography